TECHNICAL
REPORT

Options for Transitional Security Capabilities for America

Terrence K. Kelly

Prepared for the United States Army

The research described in this report was sponsored by the United States Army under Contract No. DASW01-01-C-0003.

Library of Congress Cataloging-in-Publication Data

Kelly, Terrence K.
    Options for transitional security capabilities for America / Terrence K. Kelly.
      p. cm. — (Technical report)
    Includes bibliographical references.
    ISBN-13: 978-0-8330-3929-3 (pbk. : alk. paper)
    1. United States. Armed Forces—Military police. 2. Security, International. 3. Police. 4. Nation-building.
  5. Regime change. I. Title. II. Series: Technical report (Rand Corporation)

UB825.U54K45 2006
355.4'9—dc22

2006015129

Published 2006 by the RAND Corporation
1776 Main Street, P.O. Box 2138, Santa Monica, CA 90407-2138
1200 South Hayes Street, Arlington, VA 22202-5050
4570 Fifth Avenue, Suite 600, Pittsburgh, PA 15213
RAND URL: http://www.rand.org/
To order RAND documents or to obtain additional information, contact
Distribution Services: Telephone: (310) 451-7002;
Fax: (310) 451-6915; Email: order@rand.org

Preface

This report describes the characteristics and some of the challenges of creating an American transitional law enforcement capability, then presents and discusses options for doing so. It summarizes the results of a research project called "Options for Providing Policing Capabilities in Stability and Reconstruction Operations," sponsored by the U.S. Army Peacekeeping and Stability Operations Institute. The purpose of the project was to develop this information with the goal of contributing to stability operations policy development and to the Army's developing body of knowledge on this issue. This report should be of interest to the community of government agencies, nongovernmental organizations, and scholars that are involved with, or conduct research on, stability and reconstruction operations.

This research has been conducted in RAND Arroyo Center's Strategy, Doctrine, and Resources Program. The RAND Arroyo Center, part of the RAND Corporation, is a federally funded research and development center sponsored by the United States Army. Questions and comments regarding this research are welcome and should be directed to the author, Terrence Kelly, at terrence_kelly@rand.org.

The Project Unique Identification Code (PUIC) for the project that produced this document is ATWC05154.

For more information on RAND Arroyo Center, contact the Director of Operations, Marcy Agmon, at telephone (310) 393-0411, extension 6419; fax (310) 451-6952; email marcy_agmon@rand.org, or visit Arroyo's Web site at http://www.rand.org/ard/.

Contents

Figures and Tables

Figures

Tables

Summary

Since the end of the Cold War, the United States and other Western powers, freed from the threat of Soviet intervention, have found themselves involved in an increasing number of operations requiring them to establish stability and the rule of law as part of nation-building efforts, and peace enforcement and stability operations. These stability operations often initially require the exercise of executive police powers and efforts to retrain—and in some cases build from scratch—indigenous police forces. Such efforts are typically needed during an interim period, up to the point at which overall conditions are sufficiently stable and the new indigenous police forces are sufficiently prepared to take over full responsibility for police efforts. In other words, stability operations require the United States and its coalition partners to provide transitional law enforcement (TLE) capabilities.

The United States faces certain challenges in determining how best to provide a TLE capability. The U.S. federal structure does not naturally provide for such a lead (as found in the national police forces of many other countries). Moreover, the prospect of military forces taking on this mission is politically sensitive because of the unfortunate U.S. experience during the Cold War in training security forces in South and Central America. As a result, American participation in TLE efforts has generally been as part of an international effort, usually slow in getting into the country and initially lacking in capability because policing responsibilities are contracted out to officers who come as individuals rather than as police units with a common culture, doctrine, and capabilities.

Given the post–Cold War change in security requirements, the United States can expect to see a continued need for TLE forces as part of stability operations. This report attempts to provide insight into options the United States might consider in creating TLE forces and evaluates where these forces would best be located within the federal government.

Need for Stability Police Units

This study focuses in particular on how the United States might establish some form of stability police unit (SPU), a term that refers to a type of TLE capability designed to provide police capabilities in the short term that can quickly fill the public security gap that so often exists at the beginning of a stability operation. SPUs are meant to deter normal and organized crime, control unrest, and prevent "spoilers" from hindering a country or region from moving toward self-government and stability in the immediate aftermath of an intervention. We will refer to these TLE SPUs as TLE forces.

This report is primarily concerned with TLE functions during the early and middle stages of a transitional period, as shown in Figure S.1. The transitional period refers to the time during which the United States, or some coalition in which it is a partner, transfers control of security to the indigenous government as combat or some lesser form of intervention winds down.

The first box indicates the way in which, during many operations, the locus of authority for security operations will initially rest with the military commander. Following the defeat of an enemy force or some other operation designed to establish security and permit stability and reconstruction, two major transitions may take place, as indicated by the arrows leading to the lower two boxes in the figure. The first transition occurs when control of and responsibility for security passes to the civilian authorities of the intervening power. The second transition occurs when control and responsibility pass to indigenous authorities and the international intervention shifts to a supporting posture. TLE capabilities are especially important during early stages of the transition.

Criteria Used to Assess TLE Options

To assess different options for the United States to consider in providing a TLE capacity, we developed a set of nine criteria:

- Does the option provide for the real police skills required of a competent TLE force?
- Does the option provide entities capable of filling the SPU role, rather than individual police officers?

Figure S.1
Transition of Security Responsibility and Control

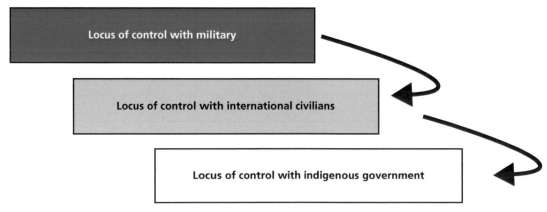

RAND *TR353-S.1*

- Does the option provide for unity of effort and the ability to work within a management structure that will ensure that TLE forces are integrated with the other rule-of-law components (especially judicial and correctional reform and development) and with other law enforcement missions (institutional development, training, and operations)?
- How well would the option work with the agency leading the U.S. element of a stability operation (e.g., military command, embassy, NATO, UN)?
- Do the proposed parent and supporting agencies have, or are they likely to have, the resources to accomplish the mission?
- What would be the option's impact on the other missions of the organization in which TLE capabilities are created—would it add to or detract from these other missions?
- What do these units do when not deployed?
- What statutory and institutional changes are necessary for implementing the option?
- How would TLE forces be supported when deployed?

These criteria were used to evaluate four options for TLE units, two of which contain suboptions. Under the Military Option, the Department of Defense (DoD) would create specialized TLE units within the U.S. military (either the Marine Corps or the Army) or provide pre-deployment training for an active-duty Army military police (MP) brigade. Under the Civilian Federal Law Enforcement Agency Option, the government would create TLE units within a federal law enforcement agency (the U.S. Marshals Service, or USMS). Under the State and Metropolitan Police Option, the federal government would fund additional positions within state and selected metropolitan police departments with the understanding that these officers will be available for deployment as part of a federal effort (which would be the responsibility of either the Army or the USMS). These officers would work in areas of their home police forces directly related to their positions in their deployment units (which would be different from the organizations to which they belong when not deployed). Finally, under the Contractor Option, the U.S. government would contract out the mission as needed (the status quo plus additional missions). Each of these four options assumes the use of contracted manpower to fill out or augment the force.

Key Findings

We assumed one year as the duration of the TLE force deployment to a given area for planning purposes. Because this report does not make a detailed analysis of all parts of each option, we do not make firm recommendations about which option the United States should pursue. However, we do present the following considerations about the options evaluated.

Military Option

Our evaluation of the Army and Marine options found that the Marine Corps fares no better with respect to any criteria than does the Army options, and worse in some. We therefore focus the discussion here on the Army suboptions. Under the Army options, success in providing needed police skills would depend on the Army's ability to recruit police officers into reserve component TLE units or to rapidly provide predeployment training to non-specialized active MP units. An Army MP–based TLE force would have some organic capability to supply police skills but not at the level required for successful TLE operations. The U.S. Army MP School would be the center for doctrinal development, training, and professional development, while the Department of Justice (DoJ) would lead other elements of rule-of-law sector in which these forces would work (e.g., judiciary and corrections). The Army option should work well with the DoJ structure through the transition, although any long-term effort led by DoJ would require significant effort on the part of both the TLE unit leaders and their higher-level commanders in the field to ensure that priorities in both military and domestic agency efforts remain focused on the goals and objectives appropriate for maintaining unity of effort in the rule-of-law sector.

This option would work well in interventions in which the locus of control for stability is with the military commander and the skills and resources exist within DoD to take on this mission. However, current limits on force structure represent a major impediment to implementing this option. The creation of an Army TLE capability would necessarily expand the responsibilities of not just that service, but also of the joint force and the entire DoD into the realm of civilian law enforcement. If the active MP brigade option were chosen, it would take one-quarter of the Army's active component MP line-brigades (based on the Army's plans for 2011) as well as approximately one-eighth of its overall deployable MP soldiers and leave an Army corps or field army without its MP brigade.

As all military forces do, Army TLE units would train while not deployed and would perform other MP functions. When under military control, the Army option would also have the most robust logistics support because it would not rely on contract assistance (other than that normally provided to the military) for essential services, and military force would be available to ensure its support.

Civilian Law Enforcement Agency Option

The USMS is the federal law enforcement agency chosen as the parent organization for this option and could provide all the skills needed for TLE functions because its officers would be involved in daily, relevant policing. Although the USMS lacks all of the organic training facilities needed for this mission, it would be capable of providing SPU-like units if given the resources to do so, and, as an operational element of DoJ, the USMS provides good assurance of understanding the demands and contributing to the unity of this effort. Although the USMS lacks significant operational experience in overseas interventions, it does have advisors in the headquarters of several such operations and is well positioned to work with a military commander when he or she is responsible for and controls security in a stability operation.

However, the addition of 6,000 TLE officers and the substantive, logistical, and administrative overhead to support them would represent a significant additional challenge for the USMS that would require substantial financial resources as well as the development of new special skills of the kind needed to conduct large operational headquarters tasks. Moreover, the potential impact on the current mission of the USMS could be significant. This apparent drawback would be offset by the significant expansion of the current size of the USMS, which would provide an increase in available personnel for domestic missions. New statutes would be needed to create a TLE force within the USMS and to permit that force to act as a component of the Army when under military control (similar to the way the Coast Guard operates as part of the Navy when under DoD control). Organic or, more likely, contracted sources would need to be created to support the force.

State and Metropolitan Police Option

This option has two suboptions in which the parent federal agency would be either the U.S. Army Reserve (USAR) or the USMS. This option, along with the USMS option, has the greatest potential to supply fully qualified and capable police officers. This is because personnel would be involved in relevant policing on a daily basis. This option could also create needed SPU-like units. However, to do so would require planning, coordination, and exercises. The USAR variant of this option would require significantly more effort than would the USMS variant to ensure that it is linked into the larger DoJ rule-of-law effort. Exercises would also be needed to ensure that a TLE force of either kind was prepared to work effectively with the agency leading the stability operation. In terms of resources, the USAR variant would have most of the same benefits and shortcomings as the military option. However, it would be better off with respect to individual training than the purely military option. As in the previous option, the USMS variant here would require substantial additional resources to establish a new 6,000-person element.

The addition of TLE forces to state and local police departments would require additional support functions but would increase the number of federally supported police officers, who would provide a significant benefit to the communities in which they work when not deployed. In other words, these officers would be contributing to national and homeland security full time, whether deployed or not.

Statutes would be needed to authorize and appropriate funds to create such a program and to permit the USMS variant to operate as a component of the military when DoD controls stability operations, as in the USMS option described above. The two variants would be supported in the same way as options using their federal parent organizations (the Army and the USMS).

Contractor Option

This option does not generally provide the requisite police skills for a competent TLE force. Unless strict contract requirements so stipulate, contractors cannot be expected to have the level of skills honed through daily training and use that active law enforcement officers would bring. Neither would these units be capable of functioning as a cohesive force unless constantly maintained as such. It would furthermore be difficult for this option to provide unity of effort with other law enforcement capabilities. Solving these problems could require the continued existence of this contract force, even when not deployed, at considerable expense.

The status of contractors would make the relationship with a military command or embassy less smooth, and the implication of a contracted force operating in conjunction with military forces also raises significant questions about the ability of a contract TLE force to operate effectively. Supporting agencies would require increases in both manpower and financial resources to meet the additional requirements of this option. Moreover, the option would create a significant new operational responsibility in the Department of State's Bureau for International Narcotics and Law Enforcement Affairs (INL), under which the current contracts for overseas civilian law enforcement fall. In addition, standing contract TLE units would not have any domestic function when not deployed. Legislation might also be required to add a significant operational component to the INL bureau.

Figure S.2 contains an evaluation of the discussion presented above using red-yellow-green color coding. Red implies that the option has significant difficulties with respect to the criteria listed in the associated column; yellow implies some difficulty; and green implies little or no difficulties, or real benefits.

Although this figure presents the results of the analysis contained within this technical report, this analysis does not include detailed cost-benefit evaluations or in-depth looks at the elements of what the military calls DOTMLPF (doctrinal, organizational, training, materiel, leadership and education, personnel, and facilities) implications. However, Figure S.1 makes clear that the contractor option fails to provide the capabilities needed, fails with respect to several of the nine criteria, and ranks significantly worse than all other options. The first figure also points out that, to be viable, a military option would need to emphasize the development and maintenance of appropriate police skills and unity of effort with the other elements of the justice system (i.e., the judicial system, corrections, and other elements of police training and institution building), primarily through close cooperation with DoJ. However, all of the non-contractor options are viable, and a more complete analysis could conceivably indicate that one of them is preferred.

Figure S.2
Summary of Options: Strengths and Weaknesses

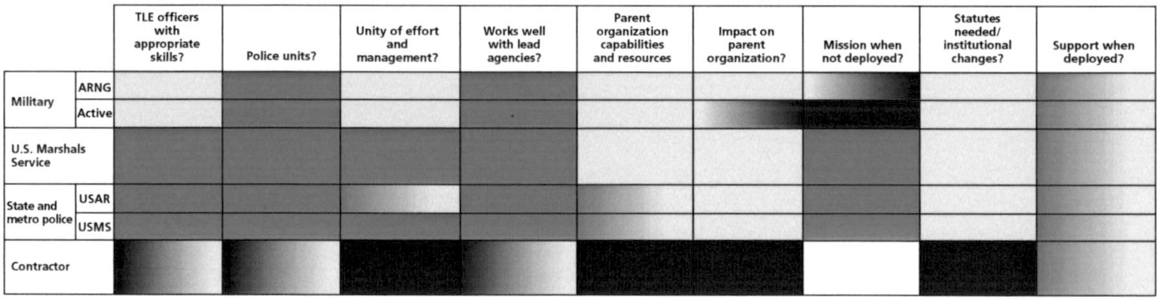

		TLE officers with appropriate skills?	Police units?	Unity of effort and management?	Works well with lead agencies?	Parent organization capabilities and resources	Impact on parent organization?	Mission when not deployed?	Statutes needed/ institutional changes?	Support when deployed?
Military	ARNG									
Military	Active									
U.S. Marshals Service										
State and metro police	USAR									
State and metro police	USMS									
Contractor										

Acknowledgments

The author acknowledges and thanks the many people who made themselves available for interviews, provided advice or guidance, and helped make this report possible. First among these is Colonel Christine Stark of the U.S. Army Peacekeeping and Stability Operations Institute, the sponsor of this research. Her enthusiasm for this effort made it possible, and her guidance made it a better report than it would otherwise have been. Next, are the many people who made themselves available for interviews, answered emails, or provided documents and direction, and collectively were essential to developing an understanding of the issues that needed to be addressed. These include Robert Perito, Michael Dziedzic, and Beth DeGrasse of the U.S. Institute for Peace (USIP); Richard Mayer of the State Department's Bureau for International Narcotics and Law Enforcement Affairs; Robert "Carr" Trevillian of the Department of Justice's International Criminal Investigation Training Assistance Program; Arthur Roderick, Assistant Director of the U.S. Marshals Service; David Brannan of the Naval Postgraduate School and formerly the Chief of Staff for the Coalition Provisional Authority Interior Ministry in Iraq; and Seth Jones and Amy Richardson of RAND. Without their assistance, this effort would not have been nearly as pleasant or the product as useful.

Special thanks go to Keith Crane of RAND and again to Michael Dziedzic of USIP, who provided insightful comments and suggestions that made this a better product, and to Kristin Leuschner, whose efforts greatly improved the presentation of this material.

Despite all of this assistance, any errors or omissions remain the responsibility of the author.

Abbreviations

ARNG	Army National Guard
CENTCOM	Central Command
CIVPOL	civilian police
CJTF-7	Combined Joint Task Force 7
CoESPU	Center of Excellence for Stability Police Units
CONOPS	concept of operations
CPA	Coalition Provisional Authority
DoD	Department of Defense
DoJ	Department of Justice
DOTMLPF	doctrinal, organizational, training, materiel, leadership and education, personnel, and facilities
EU	European Union
FBI	Federal Bureau of Investigation
FPU	formed police unit
FY	fiscal year
ICITAP	International Criminal Investigation Training Assistance Program
IDTP	International Development and Training Program
INL	Bureau for International Narcotics and Law Enforcement Affairs
IO	international organization
IPOA	International Peace Operations Association
IPU	integrated police unit
JOC	joint operations center

JTF	joint task force
LE	law enforcement
MEJA	Military Extraterritorial Jurisdiction Act
MP	military police
MSU	multinational specialized unit
MTOE	Modified Table of Organization and Equipment
NATO	North Atlantic Treaty Organization
OJT	on-the-job training
OPDAT	Overseas Prosecutorial Development, Assistance and Training
OPTEMPO	operations tempo
OSD	Office of the Secretary of Defense
PKSOI	Peacekeeping and Stability Operations Institute
POST	Peace Officer Standards and Training
S/CRS	State Department's Office of the Coordinator for Reconstruction and Stability
SPU	stability police unit
SRSG	Senior Representative of the (United Nations) Secretary General
SWAT	special weapons and tactics
TLE	transitional law enforcement
UN	United Nations
USAR	U.S. Army Reserve
USIP	U.S. Institute of Peace
USMS	U.S. Marshals Service
USSS	U.S. Secret Service
VA	Department of Veterans Affairs

CHAPTER ONE

Introduction

Since the end of the Cold War, the United States and other Western powers, freed from the threat of Soviet intervention, have found themselves involved in an increasing number of operations requiring them to establish stability and the rule of law as part of nation-building efforts, and peace enforcement and stability operations.[1] These stability operations often initially require the exercise of executive police powers and efforts to retrain—and in some cases build from scratch—indigenous police forces. Such efforts are typically needed during an interim period, up to the point at which overall conditions are sufficiently stable and the new indigenous police forces are sufficiently prepared to take over full responsibility for police efforts. In other words, stability operations require the United States and its coalition partners to provide transitional law enforcement (TLE) capabilities. The transitional period, as used here, refers to the time during which the United States, or some coalition in which it is a partner, transfers control of security to civilian authorities and, eventually, to the indigenous government as combat or some other lesser intervention winds down.

The United States faces certain challenges in determining how best to provide a TLE capability. For example, the U.S. federal structure does not naturally provide for a national police force (as found in many other countries), which might take a clear institutional lead in providing police advisors and special police units for security operations overseas. Furthermore, the prospect of military forces taking on this mission is politically sensitive because of the unfortunate U.S. experience during the Cold War in training security forces in South and Central America. Indeed, because of this hesitancy to create specialized police forces in either the military or federal law enforcement communities for overseas missions, the United States is the only country that currently uses contracted police to perform international policing missions.[2] Furthermore, the United States has often delayed in providing policing or comprehensive advisory capabilities until well into an action (e.g., Panama, Afghanistan, Iraq), and

---

[1] This is not to discount interventions prior to the end of the Cold War, such as those in Grenada, the Falklands, and Panama.

[2] Robert Perito, *The American Experience with Police in Peace Operations*, Clementsport, Canada: The Canadian Peacekeeping Press of the Pearson Peacekeeping Centre, 2002, p. 5. The United States contracts out these efforts to private firms that hire police officers for the task.

never in large numbers.[3] In sum, American participation in these law enforcement efforts has generally been as part of an international effort, usually slow in getting into the country and initially lacking in capability because the contracted officers come as individuals rather than as police units with a common culture, doctrine, and capabilities.[4]

Given the post–Cold War change in security requirements, the United States can expect to face a continuing need for TLE forces as part of stability operations. This report attempts to provide insight into options the United States might consider in creating TLE forces and evaluates where these forces would best be located within the federal government.

Understanding the Role of Skilled Stability Police Units

To gain a better understanding of the options the United States might pursue, we begin by examining the role of stability police units (SPUs). This term refers to a type of TLE capability designed to deter normal and organized crime, control unrest, and prevent "spoilers" from hindering a country or region from moving toward self-government and stability in the immediate aftermath of an intervention. Three issues are of special importance to this discussion: the distinction between SPUs and longer-term constabulary forces, the different types of SPUs used in stability operations, and the different types of police capabilities needed at different stages of a stability operation.

SPUs Compared with Constabulary Forces
SPU forces are designed to quickly fill the public security gap that so often exists at the beginning of a stability operation, not to serve as the long-term police force of an occupation (although they may remain in theater for longer periods to perform high-end police functions). In this sense, these forces must be distinguished from constabulary forces,[5] a term that refers to military forces organized, trained, and equipped for occupational duty. The premier examples of the latter are the forces created during World War II to occupy Germany.[6] Constabulary

---

[3] The Department of Justice (DoJ) teams from the International Criminal Investigation and Training Assistance Program (ICITAP) were in Panama, Afghanistan, and Iraq soon after or in some cases during the conflicts that preceded these stability operations. These teams, while making significant contributions, are not designed to provide comprehensive advisory support or law enforcement capabilities. Furthermore, in these cases ICITAP did not have the manpower needed to launch needed programs quickly (email discussions with DoJ officials, 2005). See also Robert Perito, *The Coalition Provisional Authority's Experience with Public Security in Iraq: Lessons Identified*, U.S. Institute of Peace, April 2005, pp. 5–6.

[4] Military terminology will be used throughout this text, both because the project is sponsored by the Army and because of the organizational examples provided by the European constabulary forces, in particular the Italian *carabinieri*.

[5] This term is sometimes used in the literature to indicate police forces in general, and by the military to indicate more general occupation forces.

[6] See Earl F. Ziemke, *The U.S. Army in the Occupation of Germany, 1944–1946*, Army Historical Series, Washington, D.C.: Center for Military History, 1990, for a detailed exposition of constabulary forces.

forces perform law enforcement activities as well as all other activities needed to run a country. Thus, they require the full spectrum of skills needed to manage an occupation and should anticipate being deployed until the occupied country becomes stable—most likely a period of several years. These forces are not considered in this report.

SPU deployments, on the other hand, are characterized by the early and—if all goes well—relatively short time in which they are the primary force filling the public security gap in the area of operations. These TLE forces require specialized police capabilities as well as the ability to work as an operational element in a military joint task force (JTF). A U.S. SPU capability could be provided by the military or other government agency, as will be discussed in this report, but, regardless of how such forces are organized, the key capability required by these forces is a policing, not a traditional military, function.

This distinction is important. The literature, supported by the comments of military and police officers, makes clear the differences between military units and civilian police forces in approaching stability operations.[7,8] One key difference involves the role of violence. Although joint and Army doctrine indicates that minimal force is to be used during peace operations,[9] the cultural perspective of the military is to use violence, or the threat of violence, to accomplish its mission. Police, on the other hand, although capable of using violence, typically seek to use the law and minimum force to establish security and domestic tranquility. Military and police forces also typically have different modes of operation and perspectives on the use of force. Military operations tend to be centrally planned and, in Western militaries, executed by relatively large units (compared to police forces). Military planning emphasizes the orchestration of multiple means of coercion. Police operations, in contrast, are generally planned at the local or precinct level and are executed by relatively small teams using organic capabilities, with additional force called for as needed.[10] While none of these differences should be under- or overstated, and all could be mitigated in part by doctrine and operational arrangements, these deep-seated cultural factors are important considerations in designing a TLE force, especially

---

[7] See, for example, Perito (2002) or Robert B. Oakley, Michael J. Dziedzic, and Eliot M. Goldberg, *Policing the New World Disorder: Peace Operations and Public Security*, Honolulu, Hawaii: University Press of the Pacific, 2002.

[8] MG Virgil Packett statements at the Seminar on Multinational Units held on March 30–31, 2004, by the *carabinieri* in Rome indicate that this type of law enforcement organization (multinational specialized units, in his experience) provide a unique capability not found in conventional military forces (transcript, in *Rassegna dell'Arma*, Suppl. No. 4, 2004). Also, author discussions and interviews with former senior Coalition Provisional Authority (CPA) Interior Ministry officials and senior U.S. and British military officers, January–June 2004 and April 2005.

[9] Joint Chiefs of Staff, Joint Publication 3-07, *Joint Operations for Military Operations Other Than War*, June 16, 1995, p. IV-1, contains a brief comment to this effect, and Department of the Army, Field Manual 3-07 (supersedes Field Manual 100-20), *Stability Operations and Support Operations*, February 20, 2003, contains more detail in paragraph 3-14.

[10] TLE units will need to span both modes of operation, able to operate with and as military units when faced with organized violent groups (whether criminal, insurgent, or terrorist) but operate principally as police and police trainers.

given the limited force structure available for the military to create special units and given the stated policy of the Army to rely on general-purpose forces for postconflict-related tasks, as well as the Army's hesitancy to create specialized forces to carry out policing operations.[11]

Types of Police Units Used in Stability Operations

We now consider the different types of police units that have been used in stability operations. As defined by PKSOI, USIP, and CoESPU's conference report on "Assessing the Role of Stability Police Units":

> Stability Police Units are robust police organizations capable of performing specialized missions involving disciplined group action. They have the capacity to use non-lethal as well as lethal force. The French Gendarmerie and the Italian Carabinieri are prominent examples of organizations possessing this hybrid of police and military characteristics.[12]

Given their flexible character, SPUs can operate under military or civilian control. The United Nations (UN), European Union (EU), and North Atlantic Treaty Organization (NATO) all have their own version of SPUs. In addition, civilian police forces, typically from countries involved in UN operations, are sometimes called in to support UN intervention efforts.

Formed Police Units (FPUs). The United Nations deploys FPUs, the missions of which are, first, to provide crowd and riot control (if given executive authority), and, second, to "provid[e] point security for vital facilities, protection for UN officials, prisoner transport, and other specialized policing functions."[13] FPUs also train and mentor indigenous police forces and assist humanitarian agencies in their missions. FPUs operate under the command of a UN-appointed police commissioner and so work for the UN authority in the area (i.e., the Senior Representative of the Secretary General—SRSG). Special arrangements are sometimes made to permit the commander of a UN-authorized military force to coordinate with FPUs.

Multinational Specialized Units (MSUs) and Integrated Police Units (IPUs). NATO employs MSUs, which are organized like SPUs but fall under the control of a NATO force commander. The European Union uses integrated police units (IPUs), police organizations that can be formed to carry out SPU-like roles.

---

[11] In comments made at the Peacekeeping and Stability Operations Institute (PKSOI)–sponsored Stability Operations Symposium at the U.S. Army War College in December 2004, an Army G-3 representative stated unequivocally that the Army would not create specialized forces for stability or constabulary missions. He stated that, given the limited force structure and the other commitments of the Army, general-purpose forces would handle all stability missions. These findings are generally echoed by the lessons learned from the March 2004 riots in Kosovo, as indicated in the unpublished PKSOI, U.S. Institute of Peace (USIP), and Center of Excellence for Stability Police Units (CoESPU) conference report from "Assessing the Role of Stability Police Units: Doctoral Implications of the Riots in Kosovo," held at the National Defense University in Washington, D.C., April 4–5, 2005.

[12] PKSOI, USIP, and CoESPU (2005).

[13] PKSOI, USIP, and CoESPU (2005).

Civilian Police (CIVPOL).[14] CIVPOL can refer to any civilian police intervention, but the term is most often used to indicate the police contingent deployed in UN operations. In these cases, the UN requests that member countries contribute police officers to fill the number required for an operation. Often, these are individual nominations, rather than formed police units. In general, this report focuses on capabilities typical of SPUs, but at times we will also refer to CIVPOL as typically carried out in UN interventions.

It is also important to note that SPUs built precisely on the model of the French *gendarmerie* or the Italian *carabinieri* would not be possible in the United States. SPU units from France and Italy are typically formed from these countries' respective national police forces, which are very large organizations—on the order of the size of national armies. The envisioned U.S. capability would have to be a much smaller standing formation with defined equipment and organization.

Types of Police Capabilities Required at Different Stages of a Stability Operation

A critical distinction must be made about the types of police capabilities required at different stages of a stability operation. At the beginning of such an operation, it is widely recognized that the intervening entity must quickly establish security because in all cases organized criminal groups—and in some cases insurgents and terrorists—quickly exploit security vacuums for their own nefarious purposes. In fact, these actors are often part of the preintervention security structure and so are well-positioned to exploit any gaps in public security. Iraq provides an example of how a situation can deteriorate if the security gap is not quickly filled after a government is deposed. Establishing security in the early stage of an intervention will often require police units with high-end, almost military, capabilities to fight or deter well-organized armed groups. These police forces should also have good unit cohesion and the ability to act in close cooperation with military forces. Fighting such paramilitary groups is not the job of "regular" police—no domestic U.S. police force would be expected to do so—but rather should be undertaken by specialized police forces, such as SPUs. Once the environment has been stabilized through effective action to dismantle or neutralize illicit power structures and spoilers and security is established, these high-end missions will abate and the primary focus will shift to institution-building, routine democratic policing, and the training of indigenous police forces, efforts that should remain ongoing. These tasks require a different set of skills, and do not require the same high-end capabilities provided by SPUs.[15] If done well, the shift from SPUs to other police forces (e.g., CIVPOL) mirrors this shift in requirements, though with considerable overlap in missions.

It is also important to note that the TLE mission is only one part of a larger rule-of-law effort that consists of three major components—law enforcement, the judiciary, and corrections—

---

[14] The term CIVPOL is no longer used by the United Nations. The current term of art is simply "police." However, because in this report we sometimes discuss domestic police and using "police" instead of CIVPOL could cause confusion, we will continue to use "CIVPOL."

[15] The first transition will likely be from military to civilian command over the SPUs. Then, as local SPUs are developed, a partnership would evolve, and, as locals gain proficiency, they would take on greater responsibility. These transitions will be outlined in Chapter Two.

that must develop and work together if democracy and respect for human rights are to be fostered and maintained. In each of these three areas, plans and programs must address not just operational concerns (e.g., putting policemen on the street), but also institution-building and training. These efforts cannot be disconnected or "stovepiped" if effective indigenous capabilities to establish the rule of law are to be created quickly. Unity of effort is required across the operational, institution-building, and training functions. In the words of one senior DoJ official:

> Historically, the international community has failed or been less than effective in post conflict situations because it has ... [stovepiped] the various "civilian police" missions. From the day a TLE force hits the ground, development and possibly training (in the form of [on-the-job training]) starts. While the TLE may be dealing with security issues on the ground ... someone must be managing the process of evaluating/assessing the capabilities of the indigenous force and making decisions about how to proceed programmatically ... to ensure the development of sustainable law enforcement institutions. Additionally there are often U.S. law enforcement operational and national security interests that must also be dealt with.... So, from day one potentially you have the need for a TLE, development/training experts, and operational law enforcement capabilities. In order for all three of these "police missions" to work there must be a seamless management structure and integrated command and control structures.[16]

Although the remainder of this report will focus primarily on TLE functions, one of the criteria for evaluating options will be the ability to provide unity of effort across the rule-of-law sector as well as across all aspects of developing a functional, sustainable, and competent law enforcement capability.

Purpose and Scope of This Report

The purpose of this report is to present options for the United States to consider in creating SPU-like TLE forces and to evaluate where these forces would best be located within the federal government. More detailed and eloquent arguments for the need for such forces have been given elsewhere, and to try to reproduce these here would beyond the scope of this effort.[17]

Methodology

The TLE options discussed in this report were created based on concepts currently being considered, an understanding of where the expertise to conduct the law enforcement missions resides, consideration of the criteria for evaluating options, and the status quo. This resulted

---

[16] Emailed comments from Carr Trevillian, Deputy Director, ICITAP, July 28, 2005.

[17] See, for example, Robert Perito, *Where Is the Lone Ranger When We Need Him? America's Search for a Postconflict Stability Force*, Washington, D.C.: U.S. Institute of Peace, 2004. This book lays out the case for a comprehensive stability force, including SPU-like police forces, presents several case studies to support its argument, and then provides a proposal for such a force.

in four principal options, two of which initially contain suboptions. We then evaluate these options using a set of nine criteria, which are outlined in Chapter Two. A summary of this evaluation is presented in Figure 4.1 as a red-yellow-green color-coded evaluation for easy reference and comparison.

Our review of the state of what is known about providing for TLE involved reviewing both published works (e.g., books, journal articles), unpublished works (e.g., internal government documents), and works in progress; interviews with experts in government (U.S. and others) and the private sector; and drawing on the internal expertise resident at RAND.

Assumptions

Our analysis proceeds on the following assumptions, based on stated U.S. policy and lessons learned from previous interventions:

- The personnel, organization, and equipment requirements of each option will be essentially the same. Some differences will certainly exist because of the different institutional requirements of the parent organizations, but the operational elements will be driven by requirements and so will be similar.
- The United States will participate in many stability operations in the future, and military and police skills will be complementary in these operations.
- Although the active-duty military has the ability to perform TLE functions if organized and trained to do so, the active Army structure will not include "constabulary" units or units whose sole purpose is stability operations, and in particular, active end strength will not increase to provide for such units.
- U.S. TLE personnel will be deployed for at most one out of three years on a sustained basis.
- The United States will need units resembling SPUs to be able to contribute to UN CIVPOL efforts.
- U.S. TLE capabilities will be of primary importance during and immediately after combat or other operations. They will merge with international efforts later in a deployment, and the United States will not be left to handle an intervention indefinitely on its own.[18]

Limits to the Study's Scope

The report does not attempt to articulate detailed descriptions of each option (e.g., tables of organization and equipment, cost calculations) and therefore does not provide a cost-benefit analysis.[19] It also does not present a detailed examination of the doctrinal, organizational, training, materiel, leadership and education, personnel, and facilities (DOTMLPF) implica-

---

[18] Should the United States conduct a major, long-term TLE effort unilaterally, additional forces would likely be required.

[19] A fixed table of equipment and organization would be necessary if this effort proposed to do a detailed analysis, including cost-benefit analysis, determination of the institutional support requirements, and so forth. Instead, what this technical report presents are statements about whether or not an option is feasible with respect to the different criteria that will be proposed and discussions about the difficulties of meeting these criteria. Detailed analyses will, necessarily, be left to future research efforts.

tions of each option. Because we have not made a detailed analysis of all parts of each option, we do not make firm recommendations about which option the United States should pursue.

Neither does the report attempt to provide an analytic answer about how large the TLE force ought to be. The best method of determining the size of the needed TLE force would be to use projections of future world stability and to articulate needed capabilities based on this vision, leading to a firm requirements statement. Unfortunately, such work is beyond the scope of this effort. Instead, we look at examples of requirements for similar forces and use that as a working estimate for our analysis.

Organization of This Report

The remainder of this report is divided into three chapters:

- Chapter Two examines the situations a TLE force would need to address, and discusses the characteristics and capabilities required to meet the law enforcement challenges of transitional situations. This chapter also presents the set of nine criteria that will be used to evaluate TLE options.
- Chapter Three describes the four options (including suboptions) presented for consideration.
- Chapter Four evaluates the options against the set of criteria described in Chapter Two.

What Is a Transitional Law Enforcement Force?

Before proposing options for transitional law enforcement (TLE) capabilities, we need to define more clearly the transitions involved in stability operations and discuss the characteristics and capabilities that will be required to meet the law enforcement challenges of transitional situations. This chapter also presents the criteria that will be used to evaluate the options considered in this report.

During the transitional period, it is critical to address any gaps in public security. For example, we note that while Operation Iraqi Freedom was militarily brilliant, it may not have been politically as astute because it left behind a yawning public security void that has arguably yet to be filled even as this document is being written in summer 2005. Quickly filling the security void left by a collapsing regime may be as important or more important to overall success than quick victory on the battlefield. Moreover, an understanding of the other transitions that can be expected during stability operations informs the debate about what capabilities the United States needs and, by extension, the type of police force the United States should create.

Major Transitions Involved in Stability Operations

The transitional period, as used here, is the time during which the United States, or some coalition in which it is a partner, transfers control of security to the indigenous government as combat or some lesser intervention winds down. To develop an understanding of the transitions involved, we focus on changes in control of security operations, as indicated in Figure 2.1.[1]

The first box indicates that during many operations the locus of authority for security operations will initially rest with the military commander. This would occur when military forces are deployed to defeat an enemy regime or otherwise to forcibly create the situation on the ground demanded by proper political authority (e.g., peace enforcement operations). In many cases, this stage can be envisioned as a military wave that passes over a territory, rolling toward the enemy and leaving in its wake a public security vacuum as the political structure and security

---

[1] This figure outlines a lengthy process in which partnerships between the various intervening entities, and between these entities and indigenous authorities, need to be developed.

Figure 2.1
Transition of Security Responsibility and Control

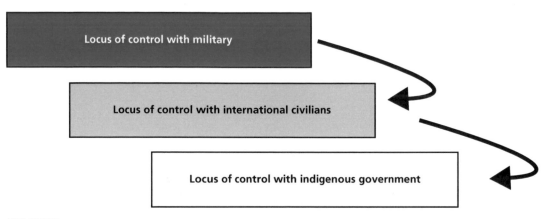

forces of the defeated state go into hiding, join resistance organizations, or simply go home. As amply documented by USIP's sequence of studies on the rule of law and security, we cannot afford a period of prolonged instability, and military forces have not been numerous enough or properly trained to restore civil order.[2,3] It should also be noted that there may be a time when the locus of control is unclear, as civilian authorities move into the area of operations and assert some control (e.g., a U.S. ambassador or senior representative of the UN Secretary General—SRSG). During this period, some functions may remain under military control while others fall to civilian authorities.[4]

Following the defeat of an enemy force or some other operation designed to establish security and permit stability and reconstruction, two major transitions may take place, as indicated in Figure 2.1 by the arrows leading to the lower two boxes in the figure. The first transition occurs when control of and responsibility for security passes to the civilian authorities of the intervening power. The second transition occurs when control and responsibility pass to indigenous authorities, and the international intervention shifts to a supporting posture.[5] It is also possible for no period to occur during which military forces control security or in which international civilian authorities do.

In this report, we are primarily concerned with TLE functions during the early and middle time frames ("locus of control with military" and to a lesser extent in "locus of control with international civilians" in the figure above). When the locus of control has passed com-

---

[2] Other scenarios can be envisioned in which the indigenous leaders and security forces stay in place and are slowly retrained or replaced, but in many cases (e.g., the regimes of Slobodan Milosevic, Mullah Omar, and Saddam Hussein) this will not be a viable option.

[3] See also Oakley, Dziedzic, and Goldberg (2002). This book traces the recurring problem of a public security gap from interventions in Panama through Bosnia.

[4] This was the case for the CPA and Combined Joint Task Force 7 (CJTF-7) in Iraq, from May 2003 to late June 2004.

[5] There may be a continued need for training and other types of institutional assistance.

pletely to civilian authorities, multinational CIVPOL under UN or other international organization (IO) control will take on the bulk of the effort. Even during these later phases, the United States will almost certainly play a role, and these same TLE forces (by which we mean SPU-type forces deployed during this transitional period) may contribute to that effort. The United Nations estimates that it can deploy CIVPOL in six to nine months,[6] given a situation conducive to UN deployments. In practice, it has taken longer, such as the 18 months it took to fully deploy CIVPOL to Bosnia.[7]

Furthermore, if the United Nations is involved from the beginning of an operation, then other countries may also provide TLE capabilities early on. In short, two paths exist through these transitions:

- UN or other IO multinational effort from the onset
- U.S.-led coalition (or unilateral) action at first, with UN or other IO support later.[8]

In the first case, the responsibility of the United States, as the likely supplier of most major combat forces, will be to hand off responsibilities to UN CIVPOL once established. This will likely be a relatively short-duration deployment, and while it is difficult to predict the exact duration, a reasonable estimate is one year. This would imply the creation of a capability to perform one full "rotation" of one-year, with subsequent teams participating on a much reduced basis.[9] In the second case, the U.S. responsibility could last longer in that the starting point of UN involvement might come some time after a U.S. deployment. In the worst case, IO involvement would be minimal, and this could require the United States to help build a competent domestic law enforcement capability on its own to which law enforcement operations could be handed over (five or more years according to common wisdom).

In both cases, the law enforcement missions after one year should change in similar ways as the need for higher-end skills among TLE forces gives way to a larger training and mentoring role, with a prolonged effort at institution-building, although delays could occur in the second situation if the level of danger in the area of operations remained high. These tasks,

---

[6] Perito, Dziedzic, and DeGrasse (2004), p. 5.

[7] The United Nations does not maintain standing TLE capabilities but rather asks member states to contribute law enforcement officers to UN efforts (although it does maintain some surge capacity). As has been extensively documented by various sources, this leads to significant diversity in qualifications and also to a slow start. See, for example, Perito (2002), pp. 1–9.

For Bosnia timelines, see Oakley, Dziedzic, and Goldberg (2002), p. 272.

This diversity in qualifications is illustrated by an anecdote related by COL Christine Stark, U.S. Army Military Police, in which one senior UN police official in Bosnia was apparently not up to the task. When asked about his qualifications, he described his decades-long career as a police officer as consisting of holding up traffic control paddles at an intersection where, twice a day, elephant convoys crossed the road—not superlative training or useful experience for running a police operation in a region recovering from ethnic cleansing and civil war.

[8] In the third case, in which there is no follow-on IO involvement and the United States would go it alone for the duration of the stability and reconstruction effort, the U.S. contribution would be even greater.

[9] There is also the potential for multiple deployments as is currently the case.

while requiring law enforcement skills, do not require the high-end capabilities of TLE units. For this reason, we will use one year as the duration of the TLE force deployment to a given area for planning purposes.

Another way to articulate these requirements is to say that the United States will need SPU-like units to deploy for up to one year at a time. Subsequently, it will need to be able to contribute to UN CIVPOL efforts. The first of these is a TLE task, while the second could involve some TLE officers but could also be handled by other organizations. This is the perspective adopted in the discussions that follow. This report will focus on how to develop these units, assuming that long-term CIVPOL capabilities will be handled either by a significantly smaller contingent of TLE forces (e.g., as part of an IO effort) or by some other mechanism, such as the current method of contracting.

The two pathways outlined above share some attributes. At the start of an operation, TLE forces will often need to operate under military control or in close cooperation with the military command. Common understandings of doctrine, culture, mission, and a host of other factors would be needed. This makes close cooperation in doctrine development and training between the military and the TLE forces important. Both cases also call for a thorough grounding of the force in the perspective and logic of law enforcement. This means such tactics as using minimum force to resolve conflicts, establishing justice and domestic tranquility rather than pursuing "victory," and performing the mission as part of a larger effort to establish a rule of law that includes judiciary and correction systems—considerations not inherent in a military frame of reference focused primarily on combat operations.

Characteristics and Capabilities of TLE Forces

Major Law Enforcement Capabilities Required
Four major capabilities are needed for TLE units:

- high-end capabilities to deal with organized criminal entities, terrorists, and insurgents (though if the problems from these latter groups are too significant, military support will also be needed), including such skills as high-risk arrests, VIP protection, and the ability to dismantle high-end violent obstructionist power structures, including operations against such groups as a unit;[10]
- police intelligence and criminal investigative capabilities;
- the ability to control large crowds and potentially unruly populations; and
- the ability to train indigenous police of various types.[11]

---

[10] The term often used for these high-end capabilities is "paramilitary." This term is overused, has a pejorative connotation, and is not sufficiently well defined and so is not used here. For example, some terrorist groups are often described as paramilitary.

[11] The training mission might include running a police training base (e.g., a police academy), providing on-the-job training (OJT) through joint patrols and operations, training police leadership, and developing specialty skills. Some of these might fall to a deployable TLE unit (e.g., OJT through joint patrols) while others might be given to a CIVPOL or contracted out (e.g., establishing a police academy). As noted earlier, all such efforts should be managed by the appropriate U.S. government agency or IO (e.g., training academies would be managed by ICITAP).

The TLE force would normally not be independently responsible for policing the indigenous population, for a few reasons. First, no country should be expected to police another nation for an extended period, particularly if it has a significantly different culture and a different language. This task may be necessary for a short period of time and done in conjunction with military forces, but it very quickly must be transferred to the indigenous population, or significant additional capability will have to be fielded. Second, foreign police, particularly those from another culture who do not speak the local language, could never be as effective as trained local police. They could, however, patrol *with* local police as part of the training mission. However, capable forces, such as TLE units, may be required for such high-end tasks as combating endemic corruption in the power structures of a nation or fighting insurgents or entrenched organized crime because these tasks cannot be left to a fledgling indigenous police force without the requisite capabilities.

Other Capabilities Needed

In addition to the major capabilities described above, a TLE capability must be ready to deploy on relatively short notice because the quick resolution of an unstable situation can often stave off worse security problems later. In particular, U.S. TLE capabilities must quickly fill the public security gap often created by international intervention. For our purposes, we can take this to mean that it is deployable on a schedule roughly equivalent to that of military forces— that is, some elements must be able to deploy rapidly, others in a reasonable time, and others on a more extended schedule.[12] This also means that:

- Police units must exist as units, rather than as collections of individuals who need extensive training to build unit capabilities.
- There must be a training and doctrine development capability to ensure that TLE forces can operate up to standard, and effectively with military forces.
- There must be structures available to support them once they are deployed (e.g., food, water, ammunition, vehicles, maintenance).

The skills needed for TLE missions are true police skills. They include such tasks as high-risk arrests, evidence collection and preservation, a thorough understanding of how the police function fits into the larger rule-of-law sector and particularly how it works with the judiciary, and the ability to train indigenous police forces on the spectrum of skills they will need to sustain democratic law enforcement after the TLE force departs.

In addition, one item essential for many stability operations is the establishment of institutional training and development capabilities (e.g., a police academy, providing advisors to government ministries). These capabilities are not included in this analysis because they are largely static, long-term efforts that fall under existing U.S. government agencies or are assumed by IOs or other institutions (e.g., such UN or regional bodies as NATO) if an intervention is lead by an IO. In particular, the capability to establish and run a police academy is

---

[12] Determining this schedule is beyond the scope of this report, but military models are likely to offer good guidelines for the interested reader.

not a TLE capability for the purposes of this report (although the leadership of the TLE forces might contribute to the planning and direction of one as part of their role to mentor and train the indigenous police forces).

Size of the Force

Another consideration for designing a TLE force is the size of the force needed. To develop an estimate for how large a TLE force should be, this study looked at EU plans for its police unit because they provide a useful starting point for an estimate of total U.S. requirement. In 2001, the EU created a police unit to provide such capabilities as those that were needed in the Balkans. It is not a standing force but a pool of police forces from EU member nations that has a goal of making 5,000 civilian police available for deployment, with a 1,400-member contingent ready to deploy on a 30-day notice.[13] This 5,000-person force is composed of both SPU-like units and individual police, with the 1,400 rapidly deployable personnel belonging primarily to organizations such as the French *gendarmerie* and the Italian *carabinieri*. If one looks at the EU as a confederation of states with populations and GDP roughly that of the United States and take into consideration that the United States has truly global interests rather than the predominantly regional interest of the EU, as well as a somewhat more active foreign policy, the EU police-unit manning figure can be taken as a low estimate of what the United States would need in a TLE capability.

Another factor that will impact sizing is the policy on how often forces will be deployed, and for how long. The U.S. Army's policy is for troops to be deployed for one out of three years, and for the purposes of this report we will use the same goal for any given law enforcement officer.[14]

Using the EU figures as a starting point and assuming the need for three rotations of rapidly deployable SPU-like TLE forces, a low estimate for the needed U.S. capability is three rotations of at least 1,400 rapidly deployable personnel, or 4,200 total. Because this seems to be a low estimate, this report will assume the need for a total force of approximately 6,000 U.S. government TLE officers, plus support staff (e.g., administration, logistics). This would permit 2,000 TLE personnel to be deployed at a given time in a rotating base that would permit one-in-three-year deployments during normal duty. Using military terminology, this is a brigade-equivalent element, with some significant functions carried out by others outside this force structure (e.g., contracted help).[15]

Ownership of the TLE Capability

A key consideration in the creation of a U.S. TLE capability is which U.S. department or agency would own it. This is the fundamental bureaucratic question critical to the successful development and maintenance of this capability. The decision to place a TLE force in the

---

[13] European Union, *Declaration of the EU Chiefs of Police*, Warnsveld, The Netherlands, October 25, 2004.

[14] Department of the Army, *Army Strategic Planning Guidance 2005*, January 14, 2005.

[15] Because we are considering deployments of at most one in three years, three brigade-size headquarters might be called for. This would also provide the TLE leadership with the institutional capacity to expand the effort using police officers from other sources, such as allies, coalition partners, the United Nations, recruiting, or contracts.

Department of Defense (DoD), DoJ, the State Department, or some other agency will affect the type of people recruited, its ability to work with other agencies, its focus, and any number of other issues. The considerations associated with different ownership options will form the core of the evaluation of options presented in the remainder of this report.

Criteria Used to Evaluate TLE Options

To answer the question of who should own the TLE force and what impact this decision would have on force capabilities and characteristics, we created a list of nine criteria, which will be used as the basis for the discussion of the options developed in the next chapter. These options incorporate both strategic design principles and practical considerations. The criteria are as follows:

- **Does the option provide for the real police skills required of a competent TLE force?** This is an important criterion because, while it would be possible to create TLE capabilities in a parent organization that does not currently have them or the culture to support them, that possibility would be expensive and could detract from that organization's ability to fulfill the mission.
- **Does the option provide SPU-like units rather than individual police officers?** One of the recurring criticisms of past U.S. (and UN) deployments has been the inability of officers to function from the beginning as units. Implicit in the concept of a deployable unit is the existence of appropriate doctrine that guides how units will function in different situations, what professional development structures will be needed to enable the leaders of these units to fulfill their responsibilities, and what training and exercise regimens will be used to ensure unit competency. The ability to function as a unit is critical when supporting military operations.
- **Does the option provide for unity of effort** and the ability to work within a management structure that will ensure TLE forces are integrated with the other rule-of-law components (judicial and correctional reform and development) and with other law enforcement missions (institutional development, training and operations)?
- **How well would the option work with the agency leading the U.S. element of a stability operation (e.g., military command, embassy, NATO, UN)?** This may be critical for success, whether that organization is military, national civilian, or international civilian.
- **Do the proposed parent and supporting agencies have, or are they likely to have, the resources to do the mission?** The resources in question here include not only the fiscal, but also the management and human resources—including the organizational culture—needed to make TLE forces effective. Although such resources could be appropriated or developed, valid concerns have been voiced about how long this would take and whether institutional impediments would prevent an organization from taking on this mission.
- **What would be the option's impact on the other missions of the organization in which TLE capabilities are created—would it add to or detract from these other**

missions? If TLE units are created within an existing organization, the mission of that organization must be considered as well because introducing a major additional function into an existing agency will very likely skew that organization's focus. On the one hand, it could cause the parent agency leadership to shift some part of its attention from the missions it currently performs or the gaining organization could become dependent on TLE forces to perform its existing missions and be reluctant to give them up for overseas deployment. On the other hand, it could enhance the parent agency's ability to perform its domestic mission through the introduction of 6,000 additional trained police officers.

- **What do these units do when not deployed?** This would be a critical question in a cost and operational effectiveness analysis. While this effort does not consider cost effectiveness, two items are clear. For an option to be most beneficial to the nation,
  - Individual members of TLE units should perform missions that permit them to remain current in the skills they will need when deployed, and preferably at the unit level rather than just the individual level.
  - Individual members of TLE organizations, and the organizations themselves if possible, should perform missions that contribute in some concrete manner to the good of the nation when not deployed.
- **What statutory and institutional changes are necessary for implementing the option?**
- **How would TLE forces be supported when deployed?**

The answers to these questions will help illuminate the strengths and weaknesses of the options proposed in Chapter Three. Chapter Four will provide the results of our evaluation.

Options for Consideration

In this chapter we describe four options for TLE units, two of which contain suboptions.

- **Military Option.** DoD creates specialized TLE units in the U.S. military (Marine and Army options are discussed).
- **Civilian Federal Law Enforcement Agency Option.** The government creates TLE units[1] in a federal law enforcement agency (the U.S. Marshals Service [USMS]).
- **State and Metropolitan Police Option.** The federal government funds additional positions within state and selected metropolitan police departments with the understanding that these officers will be available for deployment as part of a federal effort (we consider two options for federal parent organization—the U.S. Army Reserve [USAR] and the USMS).
- **Contractor Option.** The U.S. government contracts out the mission as needed (the status quo plus additional missions).

Each of these four options assumes the use of contracted manpower to fill-out or augment the force. U.S. experiences in Afghanistan and Iraq demonstrate that certain tasks (e.g., vehicle support, supply, maintenance, food services, laundry) can be contracted out even under austere and dangerous circumstances. Contractor support could include intermingling contractors throughout the deployed force (e.g., as interpreters) as well as giving specific missions to contractors (e.g., the provision of logistic, administrative, and technical services). For each option, we will discuss some details of what level of contractor support would be needed. In general, however, contract support would be prearranged for each, with support provided as needed and on a deployment schedule commensurate with that of the supported force. Our discussion of the options, furthermore, assumes that certain police functions would not fall to the TLE but would remain with the extant competent U.S. government agency. For example, the responsibility for, and oversight of, running police academies would remain with ICITAP,[2] with contract personnel contributing to this effort.

---

[1] We will use "units" to designate a set-sized, deployable, TLE element.

[2] ICITAP would continue to be the lead agency overseeing all types of training because DoJ would retain the lead for the rule-of-law sector. TLE units would contribute in OJT, but not in institutional training base efforts, because these would likely be initially contracted out and eventually run by the indigenous police force or the host country's Interior Ministry.

In the following sections, we present and briefly discuss some characteristics of each option. These options are overviews that contain the major points for consideration. Detailed analysis of such considerations as skill sets, rank structures, equipment, and costs are left for future research. It should be noted that discussion of advantages and disadvantages of the options is included in the descriptions below when necessary for clarity, such as when important considerations do not fall neatly under one of the evaluative criteria. This discussion is not repeated in Chapter Four, in which we evaluate the options.

We did not develop an option in which responsibility for the TLE force resides in the State Department, as it did not seem competitive, based on the criteria we have presented for evaluating the options. Even though the State Department currently manages the U.S. CIVPOL effort and would likely lead the larger post-conflict effort, it is not as well suited as other agencies for developing a standing police force of this size and character. This disadvantage stems from the relative competencies of the DoJ and other agencies that contain large law enforcement agencies (whether federal, state, or metropolitan), as well as the role these other agencies play in domestic security (contributing to domestic security could be an important role for TLE units when not deployed).

General Differences Between Military and Civilian Options

Before describing each option, we will first describe some fundamental differences between military units and civilian police forces. All the options fall broadly into one of these two categories.

One significant difference between police and military forces is the perspective of each on the collection and sharing of intelligence and information. Military forces attempt to collect militarily useful information (e.g., order of battle, battle damage assessments, terrain and geographical information) that contributes to operational security and to destroying enemies. Determining intelligence requirements tends to be a top-down effort, in which the needs of the command usually drive intelligence gathering and analysis.[3] Information is shared on a need-to-know basis within formal classification guidelines. Police intelligence, on the other hand, tends to be focused more on investigative efforts and so has more of a bottom-up emphasis, although, like its military counterpart, police intelligence will also look at the political and military leadership structure of the "enemy." In addition to the emphasis on social structures and interconnections, police operations emphasize sharing intelligence with trusted partners who need it.[4] In short, the military intelligence paradigm focuses on traditional military considerations, operational security, and restrictions based on "need to know," whereas the civilian

---

[3] Author interviews with CENTCOM J-2 staff, April 2005.

[4] LTC Keith Robert Lovejoy, "A Peacekeeping Force for Future Operations: Another Reassessment of the Constabulary Force Concept," unpublished academic paper, U.S. War Army College Strategy Research Project, July 2003.

paradigm focuses on finding out as much as possible about the criminal and insurgent elements, distributes information more broadly (to trusted partners), and casts a wider net. TLE units would operate in both systems.[5]

Military units also have much more robust support capabilities than civilian agencies do, and so would be less reliant on contractor support. However, to fully use this capability, military TLE units would need to be supported by a larger military force with a complete logistics and support component, such as a joint task force (JTF), or otherwise have support supplied to them.

This discussion implies that a functional military TLE force would not only need an approach to security different from that of general-purpose forces but would also require changes in other larger military functions, such as intelligence, to operate most effectively in a policing mode. This is not impossible but does present potentially significant institutional challenges.

Military Option

In this section, we consider three principal military options: a Marine Corps option and two Army options—one in the active component of the Army and one in the reserve component.[6] For the Marine and Army reserve options, we assume that the service in question would create a brigade-size unit that would train primarily for the TLE mission. This unit would have 6,000 law enforcement personnel, including its chain of command. For the Army active component option, an active military police (MP) brigade-size unit would train for SPU-like duties on notification of a need, but would otherwise maintain its normal configuration. Administrative and logistics personnel would be in addition to the 6,000 law enforcement officers. In discussing each suboption, we recognize both the institutional considerations of these two services that may make them more or less capable of providing TLE forces as well as the history and culture of each service, and in particular those components of the Army and Marine Corps that could best accomplish the TLE mission.

Marine Corps Option

The Marine Corps has a long history of constabulary operations. From Central America to Haiti to China, a principal mission of the Marine Corps prior to World War II could be characterized without much exaggeration as serving as the nation's constabulary force. The Corps' hard-earned lessons from these decades of service assisting—and in some cases administering—other countries was captured in its World War II vintage *Small Wars Manual*, a classic still cited as an authoritative reference, even though it no longer carries the force of Marine Corps

---

[5] Military police units are closer to the police perspective than general-purpose military forces, but they remain military units and do not usually do routine policing. They therefore have more of a military than a policing perspective as part of their culture.

[6] Recalling our assumption that the active component of the U.S. Army will not contain "constabulary" units or units whose sole purpose is stability operations, any Army option would likely require the proposed unit to be in one of the reserve components—the USAR and the Army National Guard (ARNG).

doctrine. In more modern times, this history, and the culture it helped determine, made itself felt in Vietnam, where the Marine Corps' Combined Action Platoon program, created in mid-1965, was the first American military operation in Vietnam that showed promise of achieving U.S. counterinsurgency goals.[7] Arguably, the Marine Corps continues to focus more on political-military considerations than its Army counterparts do. Indeed, the Corps has recently begun a process to revise its *Small Wars Manual* to serve modern circumstances.

The question of whether a Marine capability would reside in the active or reserve component of the Marine Corps is an important one. The Marine Corps has no large active-duty military police equivalent force and thus has only limited organic capability to train in police specialties. Marines could receive such training at the police schools of the Army, Navy, or Air Force, as they currently do for some other specialties. As such, a Marine Corps TLE brigade, if it were to contain trained and proficient police officers, would arguably be best placed in the Marine Reserve where it could be manned by Reservists who were full-time police officers in their civilian jobs. However, it would have no active-duty counterpart. To make this work, the active-duty Marine Corps could adopt the stability mission as a primary focus, which would be in line with evolving DoD policy.[8]

Army Reserve Option

Any Army option would be based on the skills and capabilities resident in the MP corps, which we will assume is organized in a specialized brigade. Army policy emphasizes the use of general-purpose forces (e.g., brigade combat teams), but the TLE force would need trained police officers and so specialized units, or normal MP units that received special training prior to deploying. General-purpose military forces can provide some capabilities, particularly during periods when the emphasis is on using or threatening to use force against spoilers, criminals, and insurgents. However, the average infantryman is not trained to investigate crime, preserve evidence in a manner acceptable to a judiciary system, foster professionalism grounded in the rule of law, or train indigenous police forces on the full spectrum of police skills that will be needed when U.S. forces depart (to name but a few)—all skills needed for democratic-style policing. Because of the requirement for such police skills and the fact that the Army leadership has ruled out active-duty "constabulary" and stability-only forces, any Army option that takes the form of a standing, specialized TLE unit would likely be in the reserve component where, as in the Marine option, it could also recruit from existing police forces.

---

[7] Robert W. Komer, *Bureaucracy at War: U.S. Performance in the Vietnam Conflict*, Washington, D.C.: Westview Special Studies in National Security and Defense Policy, 1986, p. 113.

[8] The February 28, 2005, draft of Department of Defense Directive Number 3000.ccE, *Department of Defense Capabilities for Stability Operations*, states in paragraph 4.1: "Stability Operations are a core U.S. military mission and U.S. military forces should be prepared to undertake them. Stability operations shall be given priority and attention comparable to combat operations, and be explicitly addressed and integrated across all DoD activities including doctrine, organization, education, training and exercises, material, leadership and personnel development, facilities, and planning."

The Army Military Police School currently trains soldiers in all skills needed for the TLE mission, although the functions performed by most active component MP units do not align well with those needed for TLE missions.[9] Chapter Four of Field Manual 3-19.1, *Military Police Operations*, begins with a statement that makes this clear:

> Military police support the Army commander's mission to win the battle. They help the commander shape the battlefield so that he can conduct decisive operations to destroy enemy forces, large or small, wherever and whenever the Army is sent to war.[10]

The MP force structure not only supplies a conduit for active-duty officer and enlisted soldiers to enter reserve component units with the basic policing skills and perspective needed for these operations, but the presence of Army reserve component units in every state in the union could permit it to recruit from the pool of police officers in various jurisdictions across the country. However, to establish a TLE brigade-size unit, the MP corps would either require the additional force structure to permit the optimal level of specialization or need to curtail other missions to permit this. Furthermore, the majority of deployable MPs are in the reserve component.[11] For example, at the end of fiscal year (FY) 2007, the MP corps will consist of 50,417 deployable soldiers, of which 16,798 will be in the active component, 22,283 in the ARNG, and 11,336 in the USAR.[12] Figure 3.1 shows projected growth in the number of deployable MPs through 2011.

As such, the MP corps could field TLE units, though probably not from its existing manpower because 6,000 soldiers would constitute a very large proportion of the MPs in the ARNG, the USAR, or both. However, increases are planned for the future, many of which will be in the ARNG because of the conversion of other types of units to MP units.[13]

As in the Marine Corps option, Army reserve component TLE units, should they be created, would need to recruit from the community of civilian police officers. In both cases, this puts a strain on the civilian police forces when they are deployed. Efforts to recruit police officers for overseas deployments have met significant resistance in the past from police departments that are undermanned, and police officers who have deployed have in some cases had to resign from their civilian positions to do so.

The principal difference between units in the USAR and the ARNG is their status during periods in which they are not serving in federal operations. ARNG units serve their respective states and governors when not federalized, while USAR units work exclusively for the federal

---

[9] See Department of the Army, Field Manual 3-19.1, *Military Police Operations*, March 22, 2001, for an overview of what MPs train to do.

[10] Department of the Army (2001), p. 4-1.

[11] Deployable soldiers are, for our purposes, those in TOE units.

[12] These data come from the U.S. Army Force Management Support Agency Web site, https://webtaads.belvoir.army.mil/usafmsa/, as of June 2005.

[13] Phone interview with Colonel Dennis, U.S. Army MP School, June 6, 2005.

Figure 3.1
Growth in U.S. Army MP End Strength

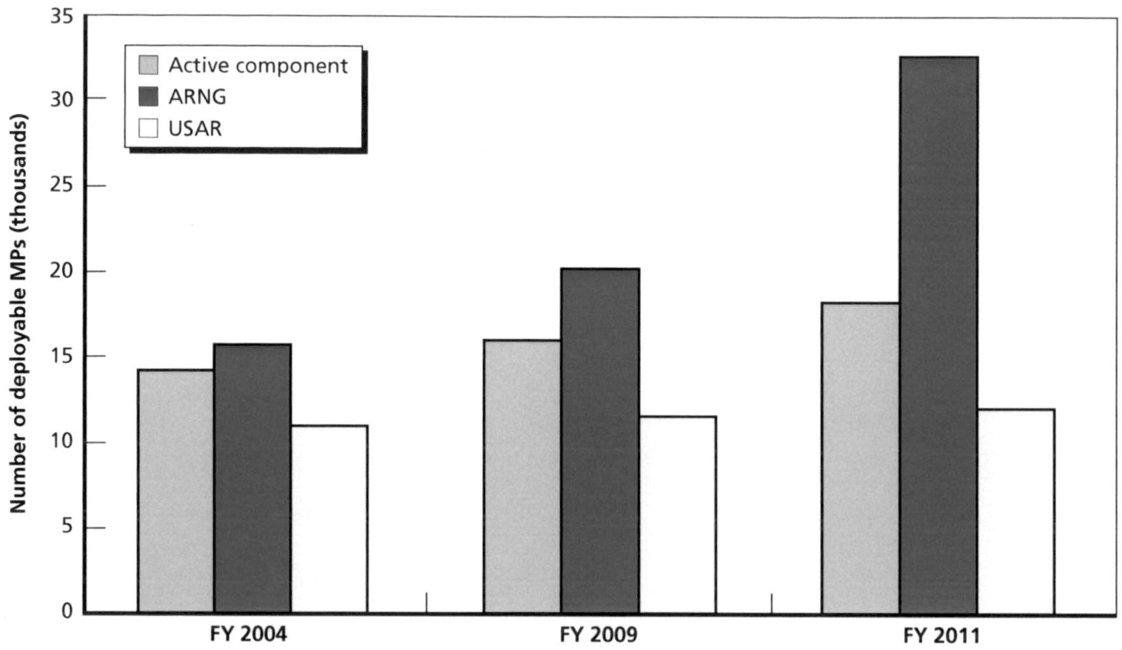

SOURCE: From "Branch Day Briefing, 11 August 2005," supplied by LTC(P) Wade Dennis, Chief of Training and Doctrine, U.S. Army MP School.
RAND *TR353-3.1*

government.[14] With the elevated concern for homeland security as well as natural disasters, ARNG MPs are often in high demand, and governors may raise concerns when they are deployed. The implications of this and other differences are discussed in more detail in the next chapter. Furthermore, USAR units are restricted in their domestic efforts by the *Posse Comitatus* Act, which does not restrict the ARNG when in state status. For this reason, Chapter Four will concentrate on the ARNG variant of this suboption.

One drawback of any reserve component option is that the presidential guidelines for the use of reserve forces stipulate that such forces will be deployed at most one year out of six.[15] That would imply either the doubling of the required number of forces, or exceptions for these types of units in which each soldier or marine in one of these units understands the deployment implications.

---

[14] Note that the Marine Corps has no Guard component and therefore no state commitment, since the states do not maintain their own navies.

[15] Lynn E. Davis, J. Michael Polich, William M. Hix, Michael D. Greenberg, Stephen D. Brady, and Ronald E. Sortor, *Stretched Thin: Army Forces for Sustained Operations*, Santa Monica, Calif.: RAND Corporation, MG-362-A, 2005, p. 40.

Active Army Option

While the discussion above correctly states the policy that the Army does not intend to create specialized forces for stability operations, the possibility exists for an active component MP brigade-size unit to receive special training when notified of the need to deploy, and thereafter to serve as a TLE unit. While not a standing specialized TLE force as in all the other options considered, this option would share some of the characteristics of the Army Reserve Option above but would have some items that distinguish it.

As an active component unit, its state of general readiness to deploy would be higher than that of a reserve component unit. This advantage would be offset at least in part by the need for specialty training prior to deployment. Most active MP units do not participate in routine or specialized law enforcement activities on a regular basis. Rather, they train to perform combat missions as part of larger Army or joint units, as do all Army units. Despite the fact that every MP gets some law enforcement training both in school and as part of his or her normal training routine, these soldiers generally do not have the law enforcement skills and culture that would be expected in an SPU. However, this shortcoming could be mitigated in part by predeployment training. Some predeployment training is a normal component of any Army unit's routine prior to shipping out, but this would be an additional requirement. The ability to conduct this training exists at the MP school, and CoESPU is currently training trainers for many nations, including the United States. The goal of this "train the trainers" program is to help countries prepare units for international service as SPUs. For units preparing to deploy on UN missions, a training period of about two months is typically required to bring units up to UN standards.

If the Army were to adopt this option, deploying up to 2,000 MPs at any time would represent a fairly large percentage of the Army's active-duty deployable MP strength. According to Figure 3.1, the active deployable MP strength will be 16,798 soldiers in fiscal year 2011, so this TLE function would represent almost one-eighth of that deployable manpower—a substantial investment. Additionally, current Army plans call for only six regular MP brigades in the Army inventory (four in the active component, two in the reserve components), roughly one per Army corps and field army.[16] Diverting one of these four active brigades would leave one of these major Army units without a key subordinate command.

---

[16] These figures come from the results of Total Army Analysis 11, meaning these are the plans for the force in 2011, and come from a briefing by Daniel C. Waddle, "Military Police (SRC 19) Card Catalog of Allocation Rules," briefing, U.S. Army Military Police School, March 2005. Other specialty MP units exist, such as those that deal with prisoners of war, but these are not considered.

U.S. Government Civilian Law Enforcement Agency Option

Several federal agencies have law enforcement capabilities, ranging from the U.S. Park Police of the Department of the Interior to the Federal Bureau of Investigation (FBI) of DoJ.[17] Because of its capabilities, the institutional powers it enjoys, and the requirements of TLE, we will limit our attention to the USMS of DoJ.[18]

The USMS has a host of police specialties ranging from special operations, high-risk arrests, and antiterrorism to witness protection, and it has the training infrastructure to support them. These would be directly useful or easily transferable to TLE missions (see the Appendix). Furthermore, the USMS has the broadest jurisdiction of any federal law enforcement agency, giving it the ability to deputize other law enforcement officers. This capability could be critical in situations in which it was necessary to rapidly expand the TLE function by bringing in police officers from outside the organization and giving them the authority and legal protections of federal marshals.

Locating the TLE force in the USMS would make for easier coordination among, and unified effort with, the other two elements of the rule-of-law sector working under the leadership of DoJ. The other elements—judicial and prison systems—fall under the International Development and Training Program (IDTP) of the Criminal Division of the DoJ (two of its offices are the International Criminal Investigation Training Assistance Program [ICITAP] and the Overseas Prosecutorial Development, Assistance and Training [OPDAT] program). Additionally, comprehensive law enforcement training also falls under ICITAP, thus providing unity of effort within law enforcement, as well as the broader rule-of-law sector.[19]

Support functions for this option could be created within the USMS, contracted out, or accomplished by some combination of USMS and contract options. For this effort, we assume that it would be contracted out, as is much of the support of all civilian agencies.

An option that should be considered if TLE forces were created in the USMS (or in any non-DoD federal agency) is a law permitting them to become elements of the Army, similar to that which makes the Coast Guard an element of the Navy when so designated by the President. This option would place the TLE forces under the same legal restrictions and

---

[17] The creation of a standing *gendarmerie* in a federal law enforcement agency has been discussed in the past. USIP's *Building Civilian Capacity for U.S. Stability Operations* (2004) presents a broad overview. More detailed analysis has been conducted by various organizations, and the U.S. government recently considered the question as part of the process that led to the establishment of the State Department's Office of the Coordinator for Reconstruction and Stability (S/CRS). In support of this effort, Michael Dziedzic and Beth DeGrasse of USIP prepared an unpublished concept paper that was a more detailed consideration of the issues that appear in *Building Civilian Capacity for U.S. Stability Operations*. The Appendix of this document is an excerpt from that paper.

[18] Arguments have been made in the past by senior Treasury Department officials that the U.S. Secret Service (USSS—then part of the Department of Treasury) would be a better choice for this role than the USMS. This is contrary to the opinions of experts interviewed as part of this research. See the summary of service capabilities in Appendix B for a further justification for not including a USSS option in this analysis.

[19] An argument could be made for placing this capability under ICITAP in the Criminal Division of DoJ because it falls under the IDTP, the division charged with international programs, including those that would work to establish functional judicial and corrections systems. IDTP could also be an option for the TLE parent organization. However, IDTP and ICITAP have no operational police force into which to integrate a TLE force and so would be forced to create one.

would provide the same legal protections afforded to the services by DoD (e.g., the protections afforded combatants under the Geneva Convention).[20] Similar legislation would help integrate the TLE force into the military early in some interventions and would affect such critical aspects as how the force could be used when deployed.

State and Metropolitan Police Option

The state and metropolitan police option consists of a brigade-size unit manned by police officers from state and metropolitan police forces. This option has two variants—one in which the federal parent agency is the USAR and one in which the federal parent agency is the USMS. This option was created to address three of the considerations mentioned above: the need for skilled police officers, for functional units, and for TLE units or personnel to have a clear and useful function when not deployed.

To create these capabilities in TLE units manned by officers from state and metropolitan police forces, the federal government needs to address two major issues: personnel and structure. It would address the first by funding additional police billets and officers in state and metropolitan police departments, with the understanding that these officers would be federalized when needed for TLE functions. The federal government would pay for these additional officers, with the requirement that they be trained in those skills needed for TLE operations and have the personnel qualifications for inclusion in this force (e.g., meet physical fitness and health criteria). Additional police billets would be spread across all participating jurisdictions. For example, if 6,000 police positions were needed, then on average, each jurisdiction could expect something less than 100 additional positions, with appropriate adjustments made to the jurisdiction-by-jurisdiction allocation based on such variables as population, anticipated threat from terrorist attacks, and other reasonable considerations. According to these agreements between the federal government and the state and metropolitan governments, these police officers would perform duties in their domestic jobs similar to those they might encounter in a TLE deployment (e.g., investigations, SWAT team) rather than being dispersed randomly throughout the parent police force according to local needs.[21]

The structure for deploying these officers would need to be carefully thought out to provide cohesion in their deployment units and minimize disruption to their home police forces. A jurisdiction could expect a structure that would not have its entire contingent of TLE offi-

---

[20] 14 USC, Section 3, states that "Upon the declaration of war or when the President directs, the Coast Guard shall operate as a service in the Navy, and shall so continue until the President, by Executive order, transfers the Coast Guard back to the Department of Homeland Security. While operating as a service in the Navy, the Coast Guard shall be subject to the orders of the Secretary of the Navy who may order changes in Coast Guard operations to render them uniform, to the extent he deems advisable, with Navy operations."

[21] Concerns have been raised that state and city governments would use funds provided for TLE police officers to offset state or city funds, thus not truly adding additional police to the rosters. While this is a possibility, recent history points out that many of these policemen would in fact be deployed one out of every three years, thus making such financial shell games unwise. Furthermore, concerns that jurisdictions would be reluctant to allow these police officers to respond when called to federal duty could be easily addressed in statute and/or budget measures, such as reduced federal funding for the state or city government in question.

cers deployed at one time, and rotations would have to be established so jurisdictions (as well as individual police officers) could anticipate when officers were most likely to be deployed. Deployment units would not necessarily be correlated with home police forces.[22] Because of the likely requirement to spread deployments across jurisdictions rather than taking all for a given deployment from a few locations, deployable units would contain members from different jurisdictions. This could be done on an individual assignment basis, by assigning small teams or units from each jurisdiction to deployable units, or by making some other arrangements to be worked out between the federal government and the police forces in question. Deployable units would be created using a model similar to military reserve units, with well-defined structures and professional leadership. This would allow TLE officers to train on doctrine as a unit, establish command and control relationships, and be significantly more effective when deployed.

This option would also have the advantage of drawing from a much larger manpower pool than would any of the options resident in a federal department or agency, including the military option. As noted in Chapter Two, the best providers of SPUs are elements of large national police forces, such as the *carabinieri*, that draw from a very large manpower pool to create SPUs.[23] The large pool of available personnel also permits units to be tailored for particular missions and spreads the hardships of deployment across a large population of police officers over the long term. No U.S. option short of creating a similar national police force could replicate this. However, in the state and metropolitan option, police officers in these units need not remain permanently in TLE billets but could rotate in and out of the rank and file of the state and metropolitan police forces, according to the policies established by the jurisdictions and the federal government. This would permit a large number of state and metropolitan police officers to get important training and experiences, decrease the strain from frequent deployments on police officers, and ensure that a cadre of knowledgeable and competent police officers would be available for deployment should a national emergency arise that required an expansion of the TLE force. Thus, a U.S. option could be made to emulate, to some degree, the manpower advantages enjoyed by the large European national police forces.

The discussion of this option is limited to state and metropolitan police forces because these officers have a more uniform level of training than is found among police officers from other U.S. jurisdictions, and organizational and funding issues are simplified by limiting the option to a small number of jurisdictions. However, there is nothing inherent to this option that would prevent other police forces from taking part. Any police officer trained to a uniform

---

[22] The way this is done will be important to the organizational effectiveness of both the deploying unit and the state and metropolitan police forces from which the units will be drawn. From the perspective of the deploying unit, placing police officers from the same police force within a single deploying unit is preferable because their daily interactions would help them to perform better as a unit. From the perspective of the state and metropolitan police forces, individual assignments would be preferable because this would minimize the number deployed at one time from any given police force and therefore minimize the effect on the efficiency of the domestic police force. Details of the method for assigning personnel are not developed here, but at a minimum, the deployable units would have a level of cohesion at least as great as any reserve component military unit and likely greater than that, because those constituting the force, even if assigned as individuals, would be working in the same field as their day-to-day jobs in their home police forces.

[23] The *carabinieri* are not part of the Italian national police force but are a separate national police entity.

standard (e.g., those established by the state Peace Officer Standards and Training commissions, duly updated to recognize the special skills needed for TLE missions) could be included if the funding and evaluation conditions were met. Note that while individual and perhaps small unit skills should be part of the local police training programs, unit skills as well as skills not used often in domestic policing would need to be part of the training given to deployable units.

The discussion thus far has addressed tactical issues of the TLE force but not its institutional structure. In particular, the force created from state and metropolitan police forces would need a federal agency as its parent organization (e.g., to supply funds and other resources, establish doctrine and standards, set up federal exercises, and absorb these police units into federal service when they are sent on missions overseas). The two logical options for parent organizations are the Army (as a reserve unit) and the USMS.

If the Army were to be the parent organization for this option, the unit could fall under either the ARNG or the USAR. The advantages of the ARNG—principally that governors could use these units during domestic emergencies, and the fact that the *Posse Comitatus* Act does not apply to Guard units unless they are federalized—would no longer be as important as in the military options when the unit personnel were employed full-time as state law enforcement officers already available for state and local duty. Furthermore, an ARNG option could limit the units to which each police officer could be assigned to only those within the state in which he or she worked. That constraint would restrict the flexibility of the federal, state, and local governments to manage the manpower issues implicit in the tension between needing cohesive, deployable units and minimizing the disruption to their home police forces. The USAR option does not have this drawback and so will be the military suboption brought forward for consideration in the next chapter.

If a civilian agency were to be the parent organization, that agency should be the USMS. All of the reasons that make the USMS the federal law enforcement agency of choice in the second option above also argue for it as the logical federal civilian agency for this option. However, because the officers assigned to these units would likely operate in homeland security functions when not deployed, an argument can also be made for placing them under the Department of Homeland Security (DHS).[24] However, this argument loses much of its appeal when we note that DoJ is the federal lead agency for the law enforcement aspects of homeland security.

For this reason, the USMS will be the civilian federal parent agency of the TLE units brought forward for evaluation in Chapter Four. Because this is the case, we will assume that the DoJ, supported by the State Department and DoD, would be the lead agency for developing doctrine, ensuring uniform training and organizing exercises as part of the larger rule-of-law sector and general stability efforts.

Before leaving this option, additional considerations are worth mentioning. First, because these police officers work for state governors and mayors when not in federal service, this option will suffer from some of the same constraints discussed under the ARNG option above—

---

[24] The TLE skills previously alluded to that require training while on domestic duty align closely with homeland security functions (e.g., high-risk arrests, anti- and counterterrorism operations, and intelligence functions).

most important, the reluctance of governors and mayors to see these officers federalized and deployed. Second, if TLE units were deployed during a conflict to provide security in the wake of advancing military forces, they would need to act in close cooperation with and under the direction of the military. Under this option, they could move initially into the USMS when federalized and then into the military structure as part of a deployed combat force in a manner similar to the U.S. Coast Guard's when acting as part of the Navy. The TLE force would then revert to DoJ service as the locus of responsibility for security passed from military to civilian control.

Support for these options when deployed would be provided in the same manner as support for the military and USMS options above because this support is external to the core TLE force under consideration here and would come from the same parent agency.

Contract Option

The Contract Option includes the status quo[25] but also builds on or leverages greater capacity in the private sector. While this option is problematic in many ways, it is included both for completeness and because of the important security functions performed by contractors in Iraq and Afghanistan.

Currently, the United States contributes to UN CIVPOL through contracts issued by the State Department's Bureau for International Narcotics and Law Enforcement Affairs (INL). INL operates as program manager, while DynCorp International (the current contractor) takes care of such operational aspects of the contract as on-the-ground leadership, recruiting, screening for physical and psychological fitness, training, and administrative and logistics tasks.[26] Once deployed, individual contractors are not subject to direct U.S. government control or jurisdiction even though they are the U.S. contribution to international operations. This is particularly troublesome because they represent the United States, and as members of an international intervention effort they may have executive police authority as well as the authority to use deadly force. Yet, there is no clear way to hold contractor employees legally responsible for their actions as police officers or for individual misbehavior, unless they are supporting DoD efforts.[27]

To date, contracts have primarily provided individual police officers with opportunities to participate in international interventions. However, the potential exists for the private sector to field formed police units. One sector expert has estimated that the industry could supply a

---

[25] Technically speaking, there is not status quo because the United States currently does not have an SPU capability. However, CIVPOL are provided by contract through the State Department, and that is the option considered here.

[26] ICITAP also provides small teams to orchestrate training in stability operations.

[27] The Military Extraterritorial Jurisdiction Act (MEJA) allows the U.S. government to hold contractors who work for DoD or agencies supporting DoD, as well as those contractors' dependents, accountable for crimes committed overseas that could result in more than one year of jail time, while leaving primary jurisdiction to the host nation. It does not cover contractors working for U.S. government agencies under other auspices. A short description of MEJA can be found in the International Peace Operations Association's newsletter, *IPOA Quarterly*, Second Quarter, April 2005.

few thousand police officers in formed units if given sufficient lead time—roughly the numbers envisioned here.[28] This option could provide one method of creating and fielding SPUs, if certain criteria could be met.

Units would have to be fixed formations for them to achieve the level of proficiency needed for the required tasks rather than formations created when a need arises. This means that the U.S. government would have to pay for them even when they were not deployed. Units might not need to be manned on a full-time basis but rather could be akin to military reserve units that contain personnel trained in their functions, with increased readiness in the rapidly deployable component.

The responsible federal agency (currently, though not necessarily, INL) would have to ensure that policing skills remained current. Ensuring that only qualified, experienced police officers were hired would be helpful, but, as contractors, members of this force could not perform police functions except when deployed, so maintaining these skills could be problematic unless the force were deployed a large percentage of the time or contained full-time police officers who agree to deploy when needed.[29]

Legal mechanisms would have to be created to provide U.S. government jurisdiction over these units when they are deployed and to ensure accountability. The problems of jurisdiction and accountability are significant when contractors are deployed as individuals, and the downside to the United States of unit misbehavior would be significantly increased when contractors were deployed as standing units with not only police skills and missions but also with the expectation that the force would have and use military skills in certain situations. Contractual assurances might not be sufficient, for example, if a criminal organization bought off a deployed unit against the will and direction of the parent company.

Now that we have described the TLE options considered, we turn to an evaluation of these capabilities.

---

[28] Interview with James Schmitt, Vice President for North American Operations, Armor Group PLC, April 27, 2005.

[29] As previously noted, recruiting from perennially shorthanded police forces is a major challenge.

CHAPTER FOUR

Evaluation

The criteria developed in Chapter Two serve as a template for the discussion of the pros and cons of each option. For ease of reference, these criteria are summarized in Table 4.1.

This discussion is summarized at the end of the chapter in Figure 4.1, which provides a clear and concise overview of the strengths and weaknesses of each option.

One item common to all options is that statutory authorizations to permit the expenditure of funds on the training of indigenous law enforcement personnel would be needed in those circumstances for which the restrictions of Section 660 of the Foreign Assistance Act (Title 22 USC, Section 2420) apply.[1] Because this is the case for all options, it will not be discussed under each.

Table 4.1
Criteria Used in Evaluation

Criterion	Description
1. TLE officers with appropriate skills	Does the option provide the police skills required for a competent TLE force?
2. Creation of SPU-like units	Does the option provide SPU-like units rather than individual police officers?
3. Unity of effort and management	Does the option work within a management structure that will provide unity of effort and ensure that TLE forces are integrated with the other rule-of-law and law enforcement components?
4. Ability to work well with lead agencies	How well would the option work with the agency leading a stability operation (e.g., military command, embassy, UN)?
5. Parent organization capabilities and resources	Do the parent and supporting agencies have, or are they likely to have, the resources to do the mission?
6. Impact on parent organization	What would be the option's impact on the other missions of the organization in which TLE capabilities are created—would it add to or detract from these other missions?
7. Mission when not deployed	What do these units do when not deployed?
8. Statutory and institutional changes needed to implement	What statutory and institutional changes are necessary for implementing the option?
9. Support when deployed	How would TLE forces be supported when deployed?

---

[1] Although, see 22 USC, Section 2420, "Police Training Prohibition," paragraph (b), for exceptions that permit training assistance in some circumstances.

Military Option

Some considerations will be common to both the Army and Marine Corps options. When operating in conjunction with general military forces, either under military command or with military forces supporting police forces, these units would be operating within their culture under the guidance of doctrine fully coordinated within their military services and the joint community and would suffer few of the disconnects common between police and military units in stability operations. This would be helpful in the early stages of a stability operation during which the military is responsible for and controls security and in other military-centric operations when control rests with civilian authorities. Furthermore, the well-developed professional military education, leader development and training and exercise systems, and assurance of full material support in equipping the force would help ensure a professional force ready to operate in stability operations alongside military combat units. As a result, this option would provide TLE units that were well trained in military functions and available for deployment on short notice. A fully mature support structure across all functions (e.g., personnel, pay, logistics, retirement, and survivor benefits) would be in place to support the TLE force when training and deployed, and would provide benefits for the families of TLE officers killed in action. Under this option, significant statutory machinery already exists to provide TLE unit members with protection when they are deployed as part of a military force and provide for the needs of individual soldiers and their families through DoD, Department of Veterans Affairs (VA), and Social Security programs. By design, these units would also fit into military support structures, though work would be needed to ensure they could continue to operate should the support responsibility shift to civilian authorities.

In all three of these suboptions, the contracted component would be minimal. Military units are designed to work as part of a military structure. As such, they include the ability to either provide for their own administrative and logistical functions (e.g., food and water, supplies, vehicle and weapons maintenance) or fit into existing structures that do because contractors cannot be expected to deploy into combat.

Turning to the criteria established for evaluating each option, we see that the Marine Corps reserve option fares no better with respect to any criteria than does the ARNG option, and worse in some. Consequently, only the ARNG option will be carried forward into Figure 4.1.

TLE Officers with Appropriate Skills

In both the Marine and Army reserve cases, success under this criterion would depend on being able to recruit police officers into reserve TLE units. An Army Reserve MP-based TLE force would have some organic capability to supply police skills because a portion of the TLE force could come from former active-duty MPs, but this would not provide the level of policing skills required for successful TLE operations. Furthermore, the Army MP School teaches all the required skills. However, the missions for which most MP units train for do not match well with those of TLE, and so MP units, although better prepared for TLE missions than other units, are not as capable as SPUs. Similarly, an active component Army MP-based TLE force would have some policing skills, but for these reasons, additional predeployment training would be required. Because the training regime to convert a line MP brigade into an SPU-like force does not currently exist, the exact duration of that training can only be approximated. One reasonable estimate might be an amount of time similar to that needed to bring reserve component units up to readiness standards prior to deployment because the tasks required are similar: individual training, followed by small-unit and battalion/brigade exercises in these new functions, would be required.

Without a sizable active-duty MP force, the Marine Corps option depends on other services for professional development and training. And because it has no active duty "parent" community to oversee and support the TLE force, it would have further institutional problems with fielding a TLE brigade. This makes the Marine option more difficult to sustain and support.

Creation of SPU-Like Units

All three military options provide units, but their ability to develop doctrine and provide appropriate professional development varies. The U.S. Army MP School would be the center for doctrinal development, training, and professional development for the Army.[2]

The Marine Corps has no equivalent schoolhouse or police-oriented doctrine and training center. While the Marines could use the Army MP School to provide some of these capabilities, the fact that the Army would not have this mission—and so would not have the resources in place to support the Marines in it—makes for a situation in which the institutional Marine Corps would have difficulty training and providing doctrine for a Marine TLE unit.

Unity of Effort and Management

The leading U.S. government agencies for the rule-of-law sector and the overall police-related efforts during stability operations will in most cases be INL and DoJ. Any military option for TLE functions should work well with the DoJ structure throughout the transition, and in particular any training and institution building should be part of the overall, long-term effort led by DoJ. For a military force to do this would require significant effort on the part of both the TLE unit leaders and their higher-level commanders in the field, who would naturally be inclined to place immediate military operational considerations ahead of long-term interagency goals and institution-building.[3] Without clear doctrine and rigorous interagency training, senior civilian and military leaders would need to ensure that priorities in both military and domestic agency efforts remain focused on goals and objectives appropriate for maintaining unity of effort in the rule-of-law sector.

In interventions in which the locus of control for stability is with the military commander, this option provides an excellent fit. When the controlling entity is either a U.S. ambassador or an SRSG, this entity would still need to operate through a military chain of

---

[2] The MP School is not currently considering specialized TLE units or related doctrine (telephone interview with LTC[P] Dennis Wade, Chief of Doctrine and Training, U.S. Army MP School, June 6, 2005).

[3] Military commanders have in the past abrogated policies with significant long-term implications for short-run tactical considerations. See Chris Schnaubelt, "After the Fight: Interagency Operations," *Parameters*, Winter 2005–2006, pp. 50–56.

command that runs to the President through the combatant commander and Secretary of Defense. Placing military forces under the direction of a civilian, whether a U.S. ambassador or the UN-appointed police commissioner, for example, could cause legal and political problems, particularly if casualties were taken. Historically, this bifurcated command structure has had a mixed record when military forces have fallen under civilian direction, even when the civilian leader has been an American (e.g., the well-known difficulties between CPA and CJTF-7 leadership in Iraq).[4]

Parent Organization Capabilities and Resources

DoD has both a large budget and a large pool of talented manpower. The skills exist within the military to take on this mission. However, policy decisions not to ask for greater permanent end strength and the concomitant limits on force structure represent a major impediment to implementing these options. Furthermore, operations tempo (OPTEMPO) for both services is currently extraordinarily high and recruiting efforts are suffering, calling into question either service's ability to fill the ranks of a larger force, even if end strength were to be increased. Because DoD policymakers seem reluctant to increase military end strength, the creation of TLE units (in the Marine Corps and Army reserve suboptions) might be at the expense of existing units, which could have a detrimental impact on the ability of the military to perform its other missions. Furthermore, the creation of the institutional machinery to make this effort successful (e.g., all aspects of DOTMLPF) might also have to come out of existing resources. Additionally, military options would require military logistical and administrative support, further taxing existing end strength.

If end strength/force structure constraints were somehow overcome (e.g., an increase in end strength for this purpose), DoD arguably has the resources and expertise to implement either of these options. The costs of training one MP brigade-size element and supplying the support structure required to field it seems manageable in a budget of more than $400 billion, so long as manpower and funds do not have to come exclusively from the budget for the existing Army MP corps or the Marine Corps.[5]

Impact on Parent Organization

The creation of a TLE capability in any military service would necessarily expand the responsibilities of not just that service, but of the joint force and the entire DoD into the realm of civilian law enforcement. As a point of fact, the military is responsible in many circumstances for public security when it is the only force on the ground, but its record of taking responsibility for public security is at best mixed.

There would be significant implications for DoD if it were to take institutional responsibility for public security, and such a decision could raise questions about which agency should

---

[4] When the civilian is a UN SRSG, there is greater unity of command than recently experienced in Iraq. The effect of these difficulties were two organizations in Iraq, the CPA and CJTF-7, operating semi-independently and without unity of effort. For detailed discussion of these problems, see Schnaubelt (2005–2006). Also, interviews and discussions with senior CPA and CJTF-7 officials, January 2004–August 2005.

[5] This is not to imply that additional appropriations would not be appropriate.

be the U.S. government lead for stability and reconstruction by forcing DoD to take the lead in an inherently civilian role. Within DoD, it would require the development of policies and doctrine (the latter being something that should be developed anyway, though not exclusively in the defense realm) for the use of these units. In addition to the issues of force structure and end strength, DoD would have to address where the policy and administrative responsibility for these missions would lie (e.g., which Assistant Secretary of Defense would be responsible for civilian law enforcement policy, how would these forces be supported when operating outside of the area of operations of any active joint task force, would a JTF have to be established by the mere fact that such a force was deployed?).

Because the services are charged by Title 10, USC, with manning training and equipping the force, not conducting operations, a service focus would include service-specific doctrinal and training issues but not operational policy.[6] Doctrine, training, and exercise development in the Marine Corps option would be problematic because of the lack of organic law enforcement expertise. This would have to be developed within the Marine Corps doctrine and training communities, or the Marines would have to leverage this capability from the Army, the other services, or some other agencies. This could be a significant challenge for the smallest of the four military services.

For the Army, the MP School would likely be responsible for the development of doctrine, though the rest of the service-wide doctrinal community would be involved because of the link between TLE and military efforts while combat and other military operations continue. Much of this will need to happen no matter which organization takes on the TLE mission. Internationally, CoESPU is developing doctrine in conjunction with several nations, as well as implementing "train the trainer" programs. The development of training and the design and implementation of exercises would, for the same reasons, likely be focused around the MP School.

The impact of the active Army suboption, however, is potentially greater if no additional end strength is forthcoming. Diverting an active MP brigade to TLE duty would strip a corps or field army of its sole MP brigade, using one-quarter of the anticipated active component MP brigade headquarters. Even if the corps or army to which this MP brigade is normally assigned was not deployed, using that MP brigade as a TLE force could significantly increase the amount of time that Army MP brigades are deployed if one or more corps or armies, along with their associated MP brigade, are already deployed. As a branch currently experiencing significant demand, the Army would likely see this as an undesirable result.

Mission When Not Deployed

As with all military forces, the units in all three suboptions would train while not deployed and perform other MP functions. The Marine Corps and Army Reserve cases would rely on reserve component organizations containing civilian police officers to ensure that current and applicable police skills were present. The active Army suboption would not have that luxury. None of the suboptions would have a full-time effect on U.S. homeland security, though the ARNG

---

[6] In particular, see Title 10, USC, Subtitle A, Chapters 4, 5, and 6, for the roles of the principal operational players, and Subtitles B, C, and D for the roles of the services.

option could have some impact if called into state service by a governor in an emergency. The *Posse Comitatus* Act would prevent the use of active Army and federalized ARNG forces for domestic law enforcement efforts, but because *Posse Comitatus* applies only to federal Army troops, ARNG troops under state control would not be so restricted. In short, with the exception of the ARNG suboption, these units would not contribute to the security of the United States when not deployed, though they could train for their overseas missions.

Statutory and Institutional Changes Needed to Implement

This option would not require significant changes to law or other institutional change beyond those already mentioned.[7]

Support When Deployed

When a military force (e.g., a joint task force) is in the area of operations, support for the military option would flow through the normal military logistics and personnel channels. In this case, it would be the best supported of the options because military units are self-sufficient once supplies are delivered. It would not rely on contract assistance (other than that normally provided to the military) for essential services, and military force would be available to ensure higher-level support. When not under military control, a military TLE force would either require an appropriate support package to be deployed with it, or it would rely on contacted support. This would either place additional burdens on the military or cause the TLE unit to train for two different modes of support.

Civilian Law Enforcement Agency Option

TLE Officers with Appropriate Skills

The USMS could provide all the skills needed for TLE functions because its officers are already involved in daily, relevant policing, although it does not have all of the organic training facilities needed for this expanded mission. As a full-time federal law enforcement agency with a broad mission, it would have little trouble meeting this requirement.

Creation of SPU-Like Units

The USMS could create these types of units, given the resources to do so. It currently contains law enforcement elements that train with military special operations forces and could easily create a structure to meet this requirement.

Unity of Effort and Management

As an operational element of DoJ, the likely lead agency for key elements of the rule-of-law sector, the USMS provides good assurance of understanding the demands of this effort and

---

[7] In Figure 4.1, which uses a red-yellow-green color-coded evaluation scheme to summarize the discussions in this section, the highest rating of any option for this criterion is amber because of the need for statutory changes permitting the training of indigenous law enforcement personnel in many circumstances.

contributing to unity of effort. Both its law enforcement and court protection components are key indicators of its suitability. Furthermore, the leaders of USMS TLE units would understand the need for a comprehensive approach to the full spectrum of police development.

Ability to Work Well with Lead Agencies

The USMS lacks significant operational experience in overseas interventions, although it does have advisors in the headquarters of several such operations and works with foreign governments and in foreign countries on various law enforcement functions. However, as the federal law enforcement agency that does the most training with U.S. Special Forces,[8] it is well positioned to work with a military commander when he or she is responsible for and controls security in a stability operation. As part of the DoJ component of the country team under the U.S. ambassador, it should be able to work equally well under civilian leadership.

Parent Organization Capabilities and Resources

The current size of the USMS is approximately 10,000 personnel, of which 5,000 provide court security. The addition of 6,000 law enforcement officers and the substantive, logistical, and administrative overhead to support them would represent a significant additional challenge that would require substantial additional resources. In addition to financial resources, the capability to conduct different kinds of headquarters tasks (e.g., doctrine development, supervision of large overseas operations) and the special skills that this requires would need to be developed.

Impact on Parent Organization

The potential impact on the current mission of the USMS could be significant. The relative magnitude of this task would arguably distract the leadership of the USMS from its current missions and would likely require a significantly expanded headquarters component to ensure that both its existing and prospective missions received adequate attention. While the task of proposing such a structure is not developed here, any such endeavor would have to ensure that at least the same amount of attention would be paid to the USMS's existing missions as is currently provided. On the other hand, an additional 4,000 to 6,000 law enforcement officers on hand for the USMS's existing missions (assuming that at most 2,000 would be deployed at a time) would make a significant addition to its current capabilities.

Mission When Not Deployed

The apparent drawback discussed in the previous paragraph would be offset by the significant expansion of the current size of the USMS. If the normal rotation ensures that TLE officers are deployed at most one out of three years, then 6,000 additional officers in the USMS implies that the contingent available for domestic missions would almost double when the court protection component of the USMS is excluded.

---

[8] Dziedzic and DeGrasse (undated), p. 33.

Statutory and Institutional Changes Needed to Implement

Two new statutes would be needed: one that would permit the USMS to act as a component of the Army when under military control and another that would create such a force.

Support When Deployed

As noted in Chapter Three, this support could come from organic or contracted sources that would have to be created to support the force. In keeping with recent practices for civilian agencies, most of this support would likely be contracted.

State and Metropolitan Police Option

The two variants of this option, state and metropolitan police activated into either the USAR or USMS as the parent organization, are discussed under each of the headings below.

TLE Officers with Appropriate Skills

This option, along with the USMS option, has the greatest potential to supply fully qualified and capable police officers. This is because the personnel involved are already involved in relevant policing on a daily basis.[9] Providing the requisite training and maintaining these skills are elements of the design of both the USAR and USMS variants of this option.

Creation of SPU-Like Units

The creation of SPU-like units is also a design characteristic of this option. However, creation of these units would take planning, coordination, and exercises. Federal exercises would be needed to permit these forces to train in their deployment units, which would to some extent be different from their home police departments. These exercises would be needed in all options to permit TLE officers to work with their interagency counterparts in DoJ, the State Department, DoD, and other federal agencies. In the USAR suboption, special emphasis would have to be placed on operations after the locus of security control passes from DoD to a civilian authority, while under the USMS suboption, similar emphasis would be needed on working under military control to ensure that TLE units could work throughout the transitional period.

Unity of Effort and Management

The evaluation of the two variants with respect to this criterion is essentially the same as in the two preceding options. However, the USAR variant of the state and metropolitan police option would require significantly more effort to ensure that it is linked into the larger DoJ rule-of-law effort than would the USMS variant.

---

[9] To the extent that reservists in the MP units discussed under the military option were civilian police officers involved in relevant police work, they would also be qualified. However, one cannot assume that all unit members would be police officers in their civilian careers or that those who were would have relevant policing roles.

Ability to Work Well with Lead Agencies

Exercises will be needed and must be based on doctrines and policies that facilitate TLE operations. The CoESPU in Vicenza, Italy (sponsored by the G-8), is developing doctrine and concepts of operations (CONOPS) that could be leveraged to facilitate some of this work. But substantial work would be needed to integrate this effort with the ongoing efforts to build a stability and reconstruction capability for the United States. Furthermore, when federalized, these forces would have the same relationship with military, State Department, DoJ, and other agencies as would the ARNG and USMS options, respectively.

Parent Organization Capabilities and Resources

The USAR variant would have most of the same benefits and shortcomings as the military option. However, it would be better off with respect to individual training. With respect to the USMS variant (and similar to the USMS option), the resources required to establish a new 6,000-person element of the USMS are currently not resident in the USMS—both in terms of financial and other resources—and this is the largest challenge to this option. The one significant difference from both the Army and USMS options is that, to a large extent, the manpower for this function would be managed and TLE officers trained by state and metropolitan police forces. This would relieve the federal government of that burden, although the federal government would still finance, set standards for, and oversee this training. Of particular note, TLE officers would hone their individual policing skills through daily use, thus decreasing the load on the MP School or USMS training facilities, as well as TLE units, to provide meaningful training. However, although the basic and advanced police skills needed for state- and metropolitan-based TLE officers would be provided to their home police forces, the parent federal agency would have to ensure standard capabilities, doctrine, and operating procedures across state and metropolitan police forces so police officers and/or small units from more than one jurisdiction could function together, much as all soldiers and military units train to the same standards so that military units can be cross-organized and operate efficiently.

The federal government—the Army or the USMS—would also be responsible for unit-level training (supported by other federal agencies) and would have to manage deployments with all the operational, administrative, and logistical overhead this implies. While much of the logistical and administrative burden for supporting deployed units could be contracted out, the responsibility and therefore some functional capability would inevitably remain with the federal government.

Impact on Parent Organization

The addition of these forces to state and local police departments would require additional support functions but would also provide many federally supported police officers. These would provide a significant benefit to the communities in which these departments exist. Many of the same headquarters-level tasks (e.g., those previously discussed under the Army and USMS options, such as doctrine development and exercise planning) would have to be taken on by the parent federal organization. For the USMS variant, this would provide the USMS with a cadre of law enforcement officers of known quality who are familiar with the USMS and who could be quickly deputized if needed for domestic missions.

Mission When Not Deployed

Importantly, these TLE officers, paid for by the federal government, would be contributing to national and homeland security full time, whether deployed or not. This additional police capability has the potential to generate the political support from governors and members of Congress necessary for it to be realized. This standing pool of trained and fit law enforcement officers could contribute to all of the police forces that participate in this effort, not only by the addition of federally funded officers above their normal complement but also because of the advanced skills and experience that these officers would have and be able to impart to their colleagues throughout their home forces.

Statutory and Institutional Changes Needed to Implement

Other than the authorization and appropriation of funds to create this program, a statute would be needed to permit the USMS variant to operate as a component of the military when DoD controls stability operations. Legal authority to train indigenous police forces would also be required in certain circumstances.[10]

Support When Deployed

The two variants would be supported in the same way as options using their federal parent organizations (the Army and the USMS), discussed above.

Contractor Option[11]

TLE Officers with Appropriate Skills

The contractor option would not generally provide the required level of police skills. Although contract organizations frequently hire retired police officers and occasionally active police officers who are looking for a change. Unless strict contract requirements so stipulate, the personnel employed in these organizations cannot be expected to have the level of skills honed through daily training and usage as active law enforcement officers would bring or possess the accompanying required level of health and physical fitness that the other options promise.

Creation of SPU-Like Units

Even though they might be so organized, these units would not come as a cohesive force unless constantly maintained as such. If the status quo is maintained, they would not be units in anything but name because they would be recruited as individuals when needed. In this case, they

---

[10] Other considerations would have to be guarded against, such as ensuring that police chiefs and commissioners did not permit only their lesser-qualified personnel to participate in these units. Personnel qualification and screening programs, as well as other regulatory or statutory provisions, could mitigate this somewhat. These considerations could be explored in depth in a future study.

[11] Throughout the report, contracts are presented as options for fulfilling certain functions. These contracts would fall under the U.S. government department or agency responsible for the mission in question. There is no implication intended that management and control of any effort would be simply left to contractors without U.S. government management and oversight unless explicitly stated.

would not be able to deploy as rapidly as military forces. If maintained as standing or reserve-like units, they would be very expensive because they would have no domestic role when not deployed.

Unity of Effort and Management

Under the status quo with State INL as the responsible federal agency, unity of effort would take significant effort on the part of INL, the country team run by the U.S. ambassador, and DoJ because the TLE officers would not only not be government personnel, but would also have no institutional anchor into the larger DoJ-led rule-of-law effort. Should the contract authority be moved from State INL to DoJ IDTP, this burden would be significantly lessened, but the fact that the TLE personnel were contractors rather than employees would still present problems. For evaluation purposes, we will assume the status quo.

Ability to Work Well with Lead Agencies

The status of contractors would make the relationship with a military command or an embassy less smooth because contractors would not have the same access as federal employees, and because INL would need to exercise on-the-ground leadership to help mitigate this lack of access. Furthermore, the legal status of contractors could create further problems that the U.S. government might have to handle, thus potentially souring the relationship between the contract TLE force and the U.S. lead agency. However, this option might not suffer from any significant relative drop in efficiency under an international organization lead because contractors would not then be seen as interlopers in an existing government structure.

The implications of a contracted force operating in conjunction with military forces also raises significant questions. These include the ability of a TLE force consisting of contracted personnel to operate as an effective force under a military command, accountability, and the authority of a U.S. military commander to direct this force, in particular if military and corporate objectives differ or military demands are outside of the tasks envisioned by the contract vehicle. Furthermore, unity of command could be an issue if the program office remains with INL at the State Department and its objectives differ from those of the military commander. Finally, deploying contract forces as part of military units during operations could raise significant legal and political concerns about the United States' practice of employing mercenaries.

Parent Organization Capabilities and Resources

INL has a program management office to handle this mission, though it does have subject-matter expertise. Significant increases would be needed in both manpower and financial resources to meet such additional requirements as the creation of doctrine, the coordination and orchestration of major exercises and operations, and all other aspects of institutional development and operational oversight.

Impact on Parent Organization

This option would create a significant, new operational responsibility in the Department of State's INL. The significant operational aspects of TLE missions make it questionable whether or not a bureau focused on policy and program oversight could manage this operational law enforcement function without significant change.

Mission When Not Deployed

Under the status quo, this is not an issue, since the units are formed as needed and otherwise do not exist. If standing contracted units were created, as stipulated in this option, they would train at some home station when not deployed but would likely not otherwise have a domestic function that would contribute to homeland or national security.

Statutory and Institutional Changes Needed to Implement

Adding a significant operational component to the Department of State's INL bureau might require legislation. Furthermore, the U.S. government does not have jurisdiction over individuals deployed as members of these forces unless deployed in missions supporting DoD, raising real issues of accountability. Legislation similar to MEJA would be needed to permit accountability for this option.

Support When Deployed

This option would be supported entirely by contract administrative and logistics efforts.

Summary of Analysis and Discussion

Figure 4.1 contains an evaluation of the discussion presented above using red-yellow-green color coding. Red implies that the option has significant difficulties with respect to the criteria listed in the associated column; yellow implies some difficulty; and green implies little or no difficulties, or real benefits.

Figure 4.1
Summary of Options: Strengths and Weaknesses

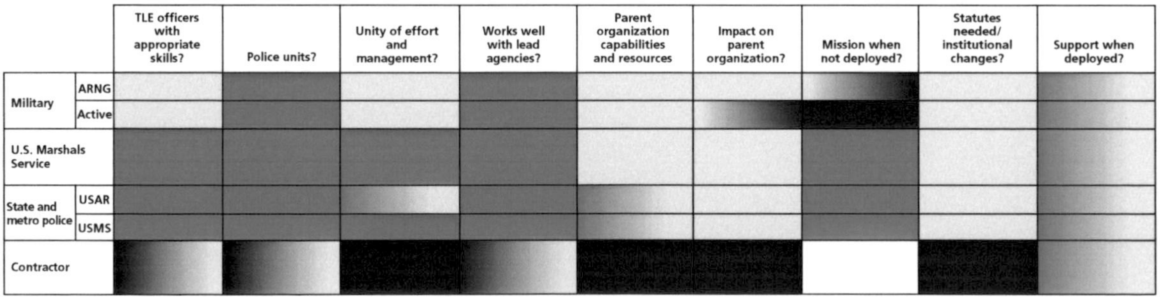

RAND TR353-4.1

In Chapter One, we mentioned that no firm recommendations would be made because a detailed analysis based on cost-benefits and the elements of DOTMLPF was not conducted. However, Figure 4.1 makes clear that the contractor option does not provide the capabilities needed, fails with respect to several of the nine criteria, and ranks significantly worse than all other options. It also points out that in order to be viable, a military option would need to emphasize the development and maintenance of appropriate police skills and unity of effort with the other elements of the justice system (i.e., the judicial system, corrections, and other elements of police training and institution building), primarily though close cooperation with the U.S. Department of Justice. However, all of the noncontractor options are viable, and a more complete analysis could conceivably indicate that one of them would be preferred.

Future Research

There remains much to be done to thoroughly investigate this topic. In particular, the range of available options needs to be expanded to include consideration of other approaches such as putting the TLE force in U.S. Special Forces, active-duty MP TLE specialized units (if the Army changes its policy on no-specialized units), or other federal law enforcement agencies. Furthermore, the major options presented above, along with the additional options that should be created, need to be analyzed for each component of DOTMLPF. This should be done through interviews with leaders in the potential parent organizations and experts in academia and nongovernmental agencies and by using appropriate analytical tools for each. Finally, an analysis of the costs and benefits of each option, as well as further investigation into the political and bureaucratic practicalities of creating each, are called for.

Federal Law Enforcement Agency Competencies

Table A.1
Agencies with Relevant Skills

Skill Sets	U.S. Civilian Agencies	Department of Defense	United Nations	Regional Organizations
Formed police units				
Crowd control	• U.S. Park Police • Major urban police departments	MPs	CIVPOL division (specialized police units)	European Union
Close protection	• USMS • USSS • Diplomatic Security Service			
High-risk arrest	• USMS • Major urban police departments			
Police				
Patrol officers	• State Department/INL (through a private contractor)	MPs	CIVPOL division	European Union
Criminal investigators	• FBI			
Border protection	• DHS			
Witness protection	• USMS			

SOURCE: Dziedzic and DeGrasse (undated).